# SUICIDE TERRORISM

IT'S ONLY A MATTER OF WHEN AND HOW WELL
PREPARED ARE AMERICA'S LAW ENFORCEMENT OFFICERS

## Anthony Davila

# ACKNOWLEDGEMENTS

I would like to express my thanks and appreciation to the Chiefs of Police for their time, assistance, and guidance. My gratitude also extends to the law enforcement officers who participated in this arduous study.

Special thanks also to my law enforcement partner and friend of many years Retired Bridgeport Police Detective Harold Dimbo.

REST IN PEACE
"SONI" & "SLICK."

Many thanks to my battle-buddies and the various veteran support organizations.

Notable mentions:
*Yolanda Harper LCSW*
*Wounded Warrior Project: Susan Deguzman*
*Semper Fi Fund: Amanda Helms*
*Director of Outdoor Odyssey: T.S. Jones,*
*Major General, USMC*

Without your encouragement, none of this could have been possible.

Finally, I would like to thank my family for their motivation, support, and unwavering patience.

# Contents

# CHAPTER FIVE

# CHAPTER SIX

# CHAPTER SEVEN

# References

*Dedicated to my parents*

# Preface

Miyamoto Musashi: One of the most skilled swordsmen in history and author of *The Book of Five Rings*. (The basis for strategy, tactics, and philosophy.)

"If you do not look at things on a large scale it will be difficult for you to master strategy. If you learn and attain this strategy, you will never lose even to twenty or thirty enemies. More than anything, to start with, you must set your heart on strategy and earnestly stick to the Way. You will come to be able to actually beat men in fights, and to be able to win with your eye. Also, by training, you will be able to freely control your own body, conquer men with your body, and with sufficient training you will be able to beat ten men with your spirit." – Miyamoto Musashi

This book is based on my thesis on how training could be enhanced by strategically integrating the existing knowledge base across all levels within emergency responders, as well as detailed knowledge of the nature and extent of the threat posed by suicide bombing extremists.

# CHAPTER ONE

## Introduction

Has anybody, at any point, considered how one individual could execute a large number of people and not feel awful about it? A huge number of people kick the bucket every year because of suicide bomb attacks; however, not very many people know why they do it. Likewise, nobody truly ponders about the past and how suicide bomb besieging began. Somebody didn't simply wake up, and choose to strap bombs to themselves, and then explode themselves inside a building loaded with individuals (Bergen, Hoffman & Tiedemann, 2011). This study will review the historical backdrop of suicide shelling, the preparation of an attacker, the identifiers of a suicide attacker, the distinctive inspirations driving his or her activity, and the way culture impacts the besieging and the attacker. Keeping in mind the end goal, to comprehend the inspirations driving suicide attacks, the society needs to get a handle on the historical backdrop of it.

Terrorism implies utilization of force and dangers against a man, groups, or governments for political or different purposes. Terrorism is not a present day movement; hundreds of years back, social orders were not as sorted out as they are today with current offices of streets, phones, and normal police compel, et cetera. At that point, head of solid groups of individuals, criminals, and warriors utilized drive and dangers to life and property to get their points. Presently, terrorism itself is a significantly sorted-out action. There are fear based oppressor associations or social orders which prepare psychological militants for their motivations. Here and there, these associations are upheld by outside governments and a large amount of resources, including sophisticated weapons, are effortlessly given to them.

A consistent terrorism association, for the most part, conflicts with the legislature. It tries to wreck key government structures, workplaces, and open spots like railroad stations and airplane terminals with bombs and damaging weapons. It executes individuals and demolishes property in crowded places like markets, transport stands, and rail stations. This sets the general population against the legislature and causes open exhibits. The impact of the bombings and the subsequent killings and devastation in various parts of our nation are a case of such fear based oppression. A fear based oppressor association working in a nation generally gets cash and weapons from the neighborhood as well as outside nations. It additionally holds hands with relevant groups who oversee the administration of the nation.

Countries or large nations utilize psychological oppressor strategies to increase more prominent flexibility or freedom. In this way, the authorities in India have been conferring demonstrations of psychological oppression to accomplish self-manages in Punjab. The Irish people in Northern Ireland have been threatening, compelling the British government to give them freedom.

There are locally-based or universal psychological oppressors who effectively capture planes or grab important or rich people. They request a large measure of cash for the release of their detainees or some political concessions for the release of the planes, travelers, or abducted people—and seizing has been very regular in our nation. Terrorism should be painstakingly checked, and the legislature ought to have zero-tolerance for the unlawful. It ought to constrain the exiles to remain in their camps constantly. It ought to embark on a course of action to stop the unlawful stream of arms and cash into the nation from abroad. It ought to have a range of truly compelling benefits for individuals who report psychological oppressor arrangements.

Different strides taken by the police or the armed forces for checking fear based oppression on an extensive scale is being talked about in the daily papers, on the radio, TV, and in some chosen congregations. According to the Terrorism Acts, terrorism openly threatens a populace, constraining an administration or global association to keep away from playing out any demonstration. It truly destabilizes or pulverizes the important political, financial, or social structures of the nation or a universal association.

In this 21st century, fear based oppression has undergone enormous or extraordinary changes due to modernization and innovations. In reality, fear based oppression exists with a broad range of causes and purposes. Certain individuals take advantage of fear based oppression to cause clashes between various groups of people and nations and once in a while, it is employed in religious differences. The psychological oppression witnessed nowadays turns out to be more savage than it used to be hundreds of years ago. Today's terrorists utilize many new strategies—for example, self-destructive attacks, remote control bombs, programmed guns and rifles, rocket launchers, and so forth, capable of causing great harm or death to a huge number of innocent people or groups. In Pakistan, the ordinary individuals bite the dust for no apparent reason—dread and fright have been incorporated into everybody's brain.

Many people groups have said, in regards to fear based oppression, as per Thomas Hobbes, who, in 1651, portrayed human life in the accompanying words: No expressions; no letters; no general public; and to top it all off, constant dread and threat of savage killing, and the life of man, single, poor, frightful, brutish and short. As indicated by Malik (2001: 88), "Endeavors to consolidate all the many appearances of fear-based oppression inside a single definition were destined from the start. The term terrorism has been connected over the entire range of political brutality, and throughout the time of history. It has been connected to times of war and of peace; to the activities of states, groups, and people; to activities against liberal states and to activities against oppressive states and tyrannies."

*Below are a few articles which are identified with terrorism:*

As indicated by Friedland and Merari (1998: 591), "Political terrorism is a modern type of mental fighting which plans to achieve political finishes by bearing on people's feelings and demeanors. This article shows the consequences of a successful sentiment study, directed on an Israeli public example, which was intended to assess the mental effects of terroristic movement and the essential suspicions that guide it. The outcomes show that psychological oppression is very viable in promoting fear and stress, notwithstanding when the actual harm it causes is direct. Nonetheless, terrorism seems to have neglected to create the attitudinal change fancied by its culprits, the large amounts of dead regardless. Unexpectedly, psychological oppression created a solidifying of states of mind, solid resistance to any type of political compromise with terrorists, and across the board bolster for extraordinary counterterrorism measures. Fear-based oppression, as it were, turned out to be counterproductive. These outcomes gave a premise to a broad examination of the conditions that transform terrorism into a possibly powerful device of political impact, and those in which it is probably going to fall flat."

As indicated by Bergholz (2006: 221), "Fear-based oppression is turning into a weapon of always expanding significance to achieve secure closures, given the capability of mass annihilation accessible to driving global forces and the ascent of one superpower commanding the common framework. Much of the time terrorism is motivated by a belief system including a worldview with superior qualities. Since these qualities are entirely consistent with adherents, they must be wanted to everything, so psychological militants are required to yield the lives of others as well as their own. It is accordingly hard to keep this sort of terrorism. Be that as it may, the undermining harms can be moderated by fiscal, innovative and political decentralization. Over the long haul, it is much more vital to winning the profound fight. This should be possible by beginning from the way that professors in philosophies whose superior qualities are clashing, can just live respectively calmly, on the off chance that they acknowledge that every individual has the privilege to pick his or her own conviction. A relating training needs to avoid fundamentalist guideline and to teach the essential standards of a free society."

As indicated by Crain and Crain (2006: 317), "In this paper, we appraise the macroeconomic outcomes of fear based oppression utilizing board information for 147 nations for the period 1968-2002. The outcomes uncover that the potential additions to a nation from decreasing fear based oppression are very substantial, in spite of the fact that the appropriate evaluations rely on upon a country's populace, the base level of yield, and venture. We display assessments of the effect of terrorism on GDP, GDP development, venture, buyer spending, and tourism. These evaluations of the minimal effect of fear based oppression give a limit against which a nation's uses on hostile to terrorism can be weighed."

As per Victoroff (2005: 3), "This article audits the best in the class of accessible hypotheses and information with respect to the brain research of terrorism. Information and hypothetical material were assembled from the world's unclassified writing. Many hypotheses and some statistic information have been distributed, however, not very many controlled experimental reviews have been led examining the mental bases of terrorism. The field is generally portrayed by hypothetical hypothesis in light of subjective elucidation of episodic perceptions. Besides, most reviews and hypotheses neglect to consider the colossal heterogeneity of psychological militants. Many reasonable, applied, and mental obstructions have impeded advance in this vital field. In any case, even as this early phase of terrorism contemplates, previous reports propose that modifiable social and mental variables add to the beginning of the aggressive psychological attitude. Mental grant could relieve the danger of disastrous attack by starting the long past due to the logical investigation of terrorism attitudes."

As indicated by Coady (2004: 37), "There are various types of psychological oppression as there are of war. It is unpersuasive to consider focusing on regular people a characterizing highlight of terrorism, and states and additionally non-state groups can take part in fear based oppression. In a majority rule government, voters in charge of an administration's ridiculous arrangements are not really honest, while recruits are honest to goodness targets. As opposed to being remarkably monstrous, fear based oppression most looks like little war. It is not generally or essentially more ethically ridiculous than war. All war ought to be dodged. However, some war is more baseless than other war. Practically same judgments ought to be made about fear based oppression.

It is suitable to think about regular citizens murdered by those looking for a political change and those utilizing brutality to anticipate such change. At times the verbal confrontation ought to concentrate on the reasonability or absence of it of the points looked for. While brutality ought to dependably be utilized as meager as could reasonably be expected, people with significant influence are in charge of making different means than savagery powerful in accomplishing legitimate political change. While considering the possible reasons for brutality, one that has gotten insufficient consideration is mortification. Mortification is not the same as a disgrace. Bringing about embarrassment can and ought to be kept away from."

Terrorism has a profound history—since the icy war—yet this issue has turned out to be the most striking after the fear based oppressor attacks on September 11, 2001. This episode influenced the UK and worldwide business groups in different ways. On the one hand, the world trade group was influenced fiscally; on the contrary, it endured because of legitimate and security issues. The universal business between nations was most truly influenced because of safety and wellbeing concerns as well as legitimate issues. In particular, the UK, US, and other nations were on impulse to secure their domain, citizens, and businesses with whatever was left of the world. Many organizations ended up wallowing fiscally for the next couple of months after the fear based oppressor attack on world Trade Center, while organizations involved in global exchange lost their own and business areas. As indicated by the U.S. branch of state (2002), more than 3000 individuals of various nationalities were murdered in the terrorist attacks in the United States alone on September 11, 2001. The attacks were the prominent case of terrorism on a worldwide level. According to the outline of the European Commission (2001), this was one of the significant occasions in the previous decades which expands the perspective and standpoint of individuals around the globe. Psychological oppression influences both the long haul and the here and now points of view of the organizations around the world.

At present, the business condition is drastically improving. The universal business in a worldwide economy has come to an end with the separation of societies. In any case, there are solid challenges against globalization, resounding its destabilizing impacts from many corners of the world. Terrorism can be seen, therefore, as one of these challenges affecting organizations. Terrorism has a number of meanings. In the realm of Alexander et al. (1979), "psychological oppression is a risk or utilization of requirement and nastiness to accomplish a political objective by methods for terrorizing trepidation, and compulsion." In the present world setting, the European Union (2001) characterizes fear based oppression, as it relates to worldwide business, in the accompanying words: "Psychological militant offenses are sure criminal offenses set out in a rundown involved to a significant degree of genuine offenses against people and property which, given their inclination or setting, may truly harm a nation or a global association were carried out with the point of truly threatening a populace; or unduly convincing a Government or universal association to perform or refrain from playing out any demonstration; or truly destabilizing or annihilating the principal political,

protected, monetary or social structures of
a nation or a worldwide association."

In the USA, terrorism is nothing new, but
organizations were rather exceedingly
influenced as a result of the September 11,
2001, and July 7, 2005, occurrences. Despite
the fact that the financial effect on UK
organizations has not been negative as at
first dreaded, it is vital not to neglect
the effect even little, unexpected expenses
can have on organizations. However, many UK
organizations were remembered that although
the obvious effect of fear based oppressor
attacks had been little, business certainty
is the key and has unavoidably been
influenced in the here and now. The greatest
monetary effect of recent year's terrorist
attacks is the harm to trust in the USA
organizations and individuals. This review
is another endeavor to look into and
research the effects of fear based
oppression on the USA organizations, and we
will likewise examine unique methodologies
for lessening and dealing with the
psychological oppression dangers.

Terrorism will turn into the new way of
fighting after the up and coming millennium

for an assortment of reasons. Since practically every nation will have enormous stockpiles of weapons, be they atomic or not, and most nations are against utilizing atomic weapons, it is a great deal more probable that militant psychological assaults and natural fighting will be used. Along these lines, psychological warfare will be utilized a great deal more far-reaching than they are direct. In response to this, security in all open and private structures ought to be significantly expanded. Be that as it may, security will never have the capacity to achieve the point where Americans are absolutely protected, and if security is sufficiently expanded to make natives feel safe, it will be excessive. This is because of the way that the vast majorities just feel safe when they are absolutely protected, and with a specific end goal to do this, it will require several security watches in each building across the nation.

Fear based oppression happens often enough in the United States to warrant solid enactment that hinders upon individual rights. Psychological oppressor acts happen so much of the time that at whatever time of

any single day anyplace, a demonstration of
fear based oppression can be seen (The
Terrorism Research Center). Extensive
enactment about psychological warfare ought
to be authorized, regardless of what rights
it infringes upon.

By 2001, the U.S. government had signs
that Al-Qaeda was arranging a large attack
on the country. However, the legislature was
not able to associate odds and ends of
knowledge spread over a few administrative
offices into a sufficiently cognizant
picture to stop the plot before its
execution. The way of the attack was
additionally unforeseen in light of the fact
that there had never been one like it. There
had been suicide bombings in different
nations. However, nobody had ever
consolidated suicide attacks with carrier
seizing. The conventional model of seizing
and prisoner arrangement was not some
portion of the agreement, and few, assuming
any, anticipated that whole business
aircraft could be assumed control and held
with things as apparently harmless as box
cutters. Along these lines, the greater part
of the world was stunned when 19 men
captured four planes on September 11,

slamming three of the planes into their expected focuses on the WTC towers and the Pentagon while the fourth landed on a Pennsylvania field when the travelers fought to retake control of the airship. The attacks brought about the demolition of the WTC towers and some portion of the Pentagon, with more than 3,000 regular folks killed. The size and extent of the operation are without parallel.

## Suicide Terrorist

Suicide bombing and terrorism have become more prevalent all over the world, not just in the United States in particular, with an increase in the number of terrorist groups. A suicide attack is a violent attack in which the attacker is expected to die during the attack. Suicide bombing has been on the increase with the growth in a number of terrorist organizations. These organizations rely on suicide bombing to promote and achieve their political agenda. Even though terrorism has been a part of the international politics for a long time, suicide terrorism is a rather new phenomenon which has been used more than was prevalent before. While traditionally suicide terrorism has been explained as one of the ways terrorists carried out the attacks, no explanation has been offered for the increase in the use of this mechanism (Reuter, 2004).

Suicide bombing is an inexpensive and efficient method for causing mass killings. These operations are less complicated, compromising, and easier to control by the terrorists than other operations that have been employed over time (Hoffman, 2003). Suicide bombing is more efficient because it tears at the fabric that holds the society together. The community is forced to struggle with the fact that some individuals consider their causes more important than life and are willing to take the lives of others in order to promote these personal causes (Hoffman, 2003). Further the society has to live with the fear of the fact that there is no easy way to defend itself against these individuals who do not only want to kill but are ready to die in the attacks, for no credible threat can be made to deter an individual who lacks the desire to survive their own attack (Hoffman, 2003).

Anthony Davila

Suicide bombing cancels the presumption of self-interest, fear of death, and rationality that fuels the market economy and the functioning of a concept of the power of the state (Reuter, 2004). The individual who is willing to sacrifice his life at the moment that his ultimate victory is achieved—for them, deterrence, retaliation, and rehabilitation become meaningless. Death has been the most powerful weapon wielded by the state and religion, which became useless after the advent of suicide bombing (Reuter, 2004). Suicide terrorism is the most aggressive form of terrorism, for it pursues coercion even at the expense of losing the support of the terrorist community. The method of terrorism has been used for demonstrative purposes or can be limited to targeted attacks. Suicide bombers seek to kill the largest number of people without discrimination, which, though effective as a tool against the enemy, is also destructive to the terrorists' cause, for people supporting this cause may get caught in the attack, leading to the cause losing sympathizers (Reuter, 2004).

The exasperating actuality is that some suicide terrorists begin heaven camps as youthful as eight years of age. This is pitiful as well as shows how society is tolerating of instructing children that it is all right for them to explode themselves, the extent of which determines the size of their nation. Beginning as youthful as twelve, children get selected for suicide attack preparation camps. Yousafzai and Moreau's article gives an inside take of a child who is experiencing the enrollment procedure (Kroenig & Pavel, 2012). His parents did not bolster the choice for him to go to the preparation camp, so the child fled to meet the spotter. When he met the scout, he was placed in the preparation camp where they showed him how to drive trucks and autos, alongside how to make suicide vests. They would likewise watch past operations of planes blowing a building or autos. Fortunately for that child, he got away from the gathering and now inhabits home with his parents. The record of this preparation indicates how crazy this thought of exploding yourself is.

So why do individuals insist and remain there? In the preparation camps, they are informed that this will make them upbeat and that they will receive the benefits in the hereafter. Likewise, they are continually reminded that this world is brimming with affliction and selling out (Dahl, 2011). As far back as the Muslim radicals attacked the World Trade Centers (suicide plane-bomb attacks), the word fanatic fits in the same class of being a fear monger. Individuals never know when a disaster—for example, a suicide attack—could happen. A few cases could be: Boston Marathon, Poe Elementary School 1959 bombing, and in 2005—The University of Oklahoma bomb incidence. Simply think of suicide bombing attack as something that could happen at any day, time, or hour. To begin off the part of a suicide terrorist, from their perspectives, is to go on a mission and slaughter their objective, murdering themselves as well. The greatest inspiration for a suicide terrorist is the despondency and misery in their lives. They likewise get persuaded in views of guarantees of an afterlife (Lankford, 2013). Suicide bombers can be of any age and have a broad range of instructive foundations. Their own lives vary and what goes on at home can be the purpose behind them becoming a suicide bomber.

The perpetration of suicide terrorism is out rightly against rules and regulations of the international humanitarian law. Suicide bombers target civilians and civilian places, and even when these attacks target the military, civilians always end up caught in the attacks (AOAV, 2015). Terrorist organizations are increasingly using children and the mentally challenged as suicide bombers. This is totally against international humanitarian law and human rights law and should be condemned fiercely.

International humanitarian law prohibits the recruitment of children less than fifteen years old by state or non-state actors for participation in hostilities. Customary international law and human rights law further protect children, whether an armed conflict is occurring or not, by preventing the recruitment of children into national armies or in taking part in armed conflicts (AOAV, 2015). The disproportionate nature of suicide bombing leading in the indiscriminate attack on civilians even when the attack was intended for the military is also against the international humanitarian law. Internationally, no law exists which makes suicide bombing illegal. In theory, a suicide bombing can be carried out within the provisions of international humanitarian law if aimed to affect combatants with no effect at all on civilians (AOAV, 2015). However, many attacks of this nature are explicitly targeted to affect civilians, which are a major violation of international law. Markets, schools, places of worship and hospitals are clearly civilian locations and have been the targets of many suicide bombers, eliminating the excuse that effect on civilians could have been accidental (AOAV, 2015). Most of these suicide bombers pretend to be civilians to gain unrestricted access to civilian objects in order to commit these attacks and in so doing, commit perfidy. Those ordering the commission of these attacks can also be held liable for the commission of war crimes under the international humanitarian law under the principle of command responsibility (AOAV, 2015).

## Background

Suicide terrorism was not very popular in the 1980s; however, after the attack on the American embassy in Beirut in 1983, there have been over 330 suicide attacks in 14 countries perpetrated by 17 organizations over the world by 2004 (Pape, 2005). Modern day suicide bombing was introduced in Lebanon in 1983 by Hezbollah (Pape, 2005). On 23rd October 1983, a truck loaded with 2,000 tons of explosives was driven into a United States Marine base in the country, killing 241 military men alongside the suicide bomber (Pape, 2005). Another attack was carried out seconds after this one on the building housing the operations of French paratroopers, killing 53 officers (Pape, 2005).

The two attacks were blamed on an Iraqi group called the Shiite military group, which eventually became the group Hezbollah. The leader of the group explained that suicide bombers were to be used where the attack was expected to bring about political change that was proportionate to the feelings that would drive an individual to use their body as an explosives host (Pape, 2005). Back then, suicide bombing was not seen as random acts of brutality but was carefully planned to achieve some mileage in political change in the direction sought out by the organizations behind the attacks.

These attacks were also directly targeted to military operations and therefore were capable of achieving the political mileage aimed at (Pape, 2005).

In 1994, groups in Palestine began using suicide bombers against Israeli targets to disrupt the attempt to restore peace in the region. Many of these attacks targeted civilians. Suicide bombing increased in Palestine, resulting in 103 attacks in the three years that followed (Morgenstern & Falk, 2009). The September 11th attack on the world Trade Centre was the biggest attack carried out by a suicide bomber on the American soil. Before this methodology, suicide terrorism had been aimed against American interests abroad, including the attack on the United States embassy in Kenya in 1998 and the attack on the USS Cole in 2000. Yet the 9/11 attacks came as a surprise, since they completely re-wrote the rules of airliner hijacking. Since this attack, suicide bombers have become more creative following the creativity employed in this attack of turning aircraft into missiles, making these attacks more innovative and destructive (Morgenstern & Falk, 2009).

After the September 11th attack, preventing terrorism became one of the main agendas of the presidency. While several measures were taken to identify who was responsible for the attack and retaliate, the citizens of the country were concerned with their security (Morgenstern, & Falk, 2009). The administration realized that their efforts at home security had to increase and cover protection of the citizens from terrorist attacks. New agencies of the government were created to improve the fight against terrorism (Morgenstern, & Falk, 2009). These included the post of the office of home security to coordinate home security agencies which, prior to the attack, operated independently. The federal bureau of investigation established the national security branch centered on fighting terrorism. After this incident, the handling of homeland security, and specifically, matters concerning terrorism, was left to the federal bureau of investigations (Morgenstern, & Falk, 2009). All cities realized their vulnerability to suicide bombing and their incapability to deal with such attacks. The cities saw it fit to stay close to federal security agencies and benefit from the improved intelligence security parameters (Morgenstern, & Falk, 2009).

It is evident that the local authorities and police officers were not prepared to deal with the September eleventh attack. Their readiness to deal with terrorist attacks, let alone suicide bombers, was not quite sufficient. The training of a law enforcement officer in America does not take into account suicide bombing, and the officers are not prepared to handle attacks of this magnitude. This study seeks to explore into what amounts to adequate preparation to equip the officers with the required skills to handle suicide bombers. It aims to identify what these necessary skills are and how they can be passed to the police officers. Comparative studies will be carried out as part of the study to determine the skills and techniques from best practices across the world.

# CHAPTER TWO

## Articles and Studies of Interest

   Several articles and studies have been
carried out on suicide bombing, addressing
different aspects of this type of terrorism.
Pape (2005) has written about the logic of
suicide bombing. In his article, Pape
explains that suicide terrorism is a
strategic move employed to achieve some
political goal. It is explained that suicide
terrorism is not the irrational actions of
an individual or the expression of
fanaticism (Pape, 2005). The attacks are
chiseled as means of exerting pain to the
receiving governments with the intention of
forcing them to change certain policies—
mainly to force democratic states to
withdraw their military forces from areas
that the terrorist groups consider their
homeland. The article defines terrorism as
the use of violence by an organization other
than a national government to cause
intimidation or fear among a target audience.

Suicide terrorism is identified as one of the forms of representing terrorism, with the other two being demonstrative terrorism and destructive terrorism (Pape, 2005).

The article sees suicide terrorism as a strategy for coercion employed to exert as much pain as possible to the opposing society to overwhelm their interest in resisting the terrorist's demands and to cause either the government to concede or the population to revolt against the government (Pape, 2005). Suicide terrorism does not apply the same way as military coercion employed by states, with the structural difference between the two making suicide terrorism a strategy for coercion. The article further explains that Suicide terrorism makes an adjustment to reduce damage more difficult than for states faced with military coercion or economic sanctions. It lists more comparison points between suicide terrorism and other tools of coercion employed by states to show the logic behind the strategy to use suicide terrorism as a coercion tool against states (Pape, 2005). The author completes his article by giving policy implications for containing suicide terrorism and starts by

pointing out that the current policy debate
which encourages the use of military action
or concessions is misguided and despite
extensive use, it has failed to achieve any
success in combating suicide bombing. He
says that homeland security and defensive
efforts are the better solutions in curbing
suicide terrorism (Pape, 2005). Despite
pointing at homeland security and internal
defending expected to be done by local law
enforcement officers, the author does not
explore how these agencies are to deal with
suicide terrorism and how ready they are to
handle this task—a loophole which this study
seeks to fill (Pape, 2005).

Pellegrini and Connors have written on the
hard worn lessons on policing terrorism in
the United States. They start by restating
the fact that local agencies are critical in
defending the country against terrorist
attacks (Pellegrini & Connors, 2005). They
also restate that the most difficult part is
identifying the practical, cost-effective
steps that will make the journey of
integrating local assets into our national
security strategy a smooth one (Pellegrini &
Connors, 2005). They suggest that this will
involve new approaches to organizing

resources, planning operations, training
personnel and multidisciplinary teams, and
developing doctrine and tactics (Pellegrini
& Connors, 2005). They further explain that
any police department, large or small, can
become more effective at prevention without
incurring substantial expenses simply by
educating themselves and becoming more
observant of suspicion indicators in their
communities. They also say that the police
officers have the duty to educate themselves
on how to deal with the modern kind of
threats (Pellegrini & Connors, 2005). They
suggest that this approach has been applied
in Israel and has helped curb terrorism in
the country. They report that the police
force in Israel has helped prevent 90
percent of the terrorist activities in the
country and suggest that if the same is done
in America, chances of preventing terrorist
attacks will be increased (Pellegrini &
Connors, 2005). While the article identifies
and supports the main point of this paper –
that the police force can play a great role
in preventing suicide terrorism and
terrorism in general—the authors fail to
identify the specific abilities and
activities that the local law enforcement
agencies need to take up in order to be able

to deal with terrorism and specifically suicide terrorism. This is the gap that this paper seeks to feel.

Present day suicide fear attacks can be characterized as rough, politically roused activities executed intentionally, effectively, and with an earlier goal of people who kill themselves while pulverizing their picked non-military personnel or military targets. Psychological militant gatherings regularly pick this strategy since it is accessible and economical, and the harm brought about to the assurance of the opponent populace is grave. A suicide attack, similar to all other dread attacks in the present day time, is intended to amplify the "control picture" of the executing association (Kroenig & Pavel, 2012). The Liberation Tigers of Tamil Eelam (LTTE) in Sri Lanka; the Palestinian fundamentalist associations of Hamas and the Palestinian Islamic Jihad (PIJ) and later other non-religious gatherings, for example, Al Aqsa Martyr Brigades and the Popular Front for the Liberation of Palestine; and the Kurdish PKK in Turkey have embraced and refined suicide attacks as their "vital weapons" against their enemies. Under Osama receptacle Laden's administration, Al-Qaeda and its partnered gatherings and systems have given a worldwide measurement to what normally seemed, by all accounts, to be national, religious, or nearby clashes.

Laden's fundamentalist Islamic belief system and his stupendous methodology have spread the suicide fear throughout the world. For Laden and his similarly invested followers, suicide psychological warfare has filled in as a weapon of insubordination and as a conventional instrument to demonstrate the amusingness of the virtue of Muslims over the debauchery of their adversaries (Kroenig & Pavel, 2012). Taking after the September 11, 2001, attacks, where surprisingly an extraordinary number of suicide attacks were utilized as a part of four synchronous suicide missions, Al-Qaeda and others have been driving a worldwide suicide battle. Through May 2004, Al-Qaeda and its offshoots had completed around 80 suicide attacks. These numbers do exclude right around 70 suicide attacks that have worked in Iraq since March 2003 (at any rate, a few, if not most, of them have a place with the "Worldwide Jihad" development) and nearly a similar number of Chechen separatist suicide attackers who began to work in 2000. Around 15 percent of suicide bombers have been ladies. A significant portion of them had a place with the Tamil LTTE or the Turkish PKK; right around 66% of the PKK's suicide attackers were female.

In both of these gatherings, their charming pioneers guaranteed the female volunteers that by taking part in the suicide crusade, they would bolster the gathering cause while demonstrating that they were as overcome as their male associates (Clapper, 2013). As of recently, female suicide attackers were special to the LTTE, PKK, and other non-religious dread associations. However, this pattern has changed as of late; some religious pioneers have purified ladies' investment in such acts under their "free" elucidation of Islamic convention. (Unexpectedly, similar men assert "strict" readings of the Koran to legitimize psychological oppression.) Thus, the Palestinian Hamas and PIJ and Chechen separatists have begun using female attackers. Essentially, those associations have been working in extremely preservationist and customary social orders where ladies have not delighted in equal

rights with men. Psychological militant
associations call upon their individuals to
partake in suicide attacks under various
flags and trademarks (Clapper, 2013).

Now and then it is done for the benefit of
God and religion, some of the time in the
interest of the "country," and commonly as a
demonstration of vengeance or prevention
against an all the more powerful for Islamic
fundamentalist associations—for example,
Hamas and the Palestinian Islamic Jihad, Al-
Qaeda, and Hizbollah conjure God and
translate the Koran in a way that fits their
political and operational needs. By doing as
such, they legitimize such a fight against
the "heathens" with regards to Islam. The
greater part of these gatherings
additionally utilizes patriotism in their
language as a rule conjuring the recovery of
a holy land having a place with the bigger
Muslim country from the hands of aggressors
(Kroenig & Pavel, 2012). As every real
religion preclude suicide, religiously
constantly expressing the intentions of
suicide attackers in "unselfish" terms,
additionally, all fear gatherings, religious
or not, wish to venture quality. Hence, the
individual thought processes of suicide

attacks are regularly hidden. Explore directed with "fizzled" suicide attacks all through the world has demonstrated that such inspirations do exist, including own mental hardships, give up and wild energy for retribution, and particular objectives of own wonderfulness—for example, familial respect or even cash for the suicide bomber's families (Kroenig & Pavel, 2012).

Asensio & Trunkey (2008) describe suicide bombing is an act whereby an individual delivers to detonate explosives to cause the greatest damage possible. It can also be defined as an action that is done violently by some offered individuals who are sure that their chances of returning to life are most likely equal to zero (Asensio & Trunkey, 2008). The people are in most cases seen to offer their lives on matters which most psychologists remain with different conclusions amongst themselves. Some research that has been conducted have placed these people more of being murderers than what is commonly thought by most of us (Asensio & Trunkey, 2008). A terrifying thing is about the people who are conducting domestic terrorism in within the United States of America without external influence

from the foreign countries. It is said that
in most cases they normally do the act out
of social and political objectives (Asensio
& Trunkey, 2008). In the process of the
individual causing the damages, he or she
also kills himself or herself.

## Review on Terrorism

Use of suicide terrorism by the terrorist
has been dated back to the ancient times
(Egner, 2009). These elements of attack are
not new in any way. The attacks had been
experienced earlier in the areas of India,
Israel and some parts of the Jewish people.
According to Egner (2009), the Muslims are
said to have been conducting the act of
suicide terrorism back in the 13th century
besides the fact that they did not have
improvised devices that could cause death to
both the victims and themselves but death
was considered part of their mission. They
used to carry out their operations in a
place that had a lot of people so that they
can publicize their acts. On their side,
they experienced suicide terrorism too in
the 18th century (Egner, 2009). The research
that was done in 2010 by the unclassified
intelligence reports clearly indicates that

the terrorism attempted attacks in the US in the year 2009 has too many comparing with any other year (Egner, 2009). The report shows that some of the terrorists are within the country and are likely to do the act of terrorism without warning and therefore the security measures of the nation should also cater for such factors like those. The report also shows that the terrorist is likely to start smaller operations that very much are likely to succeed and are less likely to be detected (Egner, 2009). These includes targets of school and retail shopping areas such as shopping malls.

As per Lennquist (2012), the suicide bombing is an act that will leave any person in a shock on the account of its indiscriminate nature, although research has shown that the target of the people who cause suicide bombing is mainly to kill the military, it has been finally noted that unsuspected civilians are the people who are mostly affected and the fact that the suicide bombers are willing to die in their own hands is a terrifying exercise. It is said that almost all the suicide bombing which happens are very much linked to political causes and it is a factor that is deliberately employed by a number of terrorists to inflict a calculated political effect (Lennquist, 2012). This is true because the suicide bombers have the right to move take security measures and perform their act of suicide at a specified target place. Research has shown that the damages that are inflicted by suicide bombing are both psychological and physical, while when the terrorists want to inflict maximum damage the suicide bombing is done as a surprise (Lennquist, 2012). For example, the terrorist will prefer to put the explosives at the back of their clothes to even cause greater damage they prefer to even drive their vehicles fitted with explosives.

The phenomenon of suicide bombing is not an act that started a long time but it is just a recent phenomenon in the US (Lennquist, 2012). Today the United States of America is facing a threat of terrorism. According to Lennquist (2012), It was back in 2001 11th September that the US faced the real danger of foreign attack. It is at this moment of time that Osama the leader of the terrorist group the al-Qaeda's declared war between their members and the US, and he said that they will not stop the war until

the time they will win it or to die in the
cause. This event indicated that these
people were very much willing to die as long
they would cause harm to the United States
of America (Lennquist, 2012). For a militant
group, the suicide bombing is not only
employed for only the reasons that are
specified above but also for more strategic
goals that are best known by themselves. It
has been referred that suicide bombing is an
issue that is difficult to stop since they
are matters that include political violence.
As per Lennquist (2012) despite the fact
that stopping suicide attacks is difficult,
there must be measures that should be put
across to protect the act from taking place.
This measures can include employing
aggressive measures on dealing with suicide
bombing or even direct attack of the leaders
of the people performing this acts. Other
measures include both defensive and passive.
This might include screening all the
vehicles and passengers or even building
high walls at the borders to avoid entry of
strangers in the country. The recent
research shows that this method has been
used several times in Israel and was seen to
curb the issue of terrorism in the country.
It is recorded that around 89% of terrorist

issues in the country has been reduced using this method and it is said that if this method is employed in America the terrorist activity is likely to reduce even more (Lennquist' 2012). Although, the article states that this method is going to reduce the rate of terrorism and more the suicide terrorism, the writers fail to explain how this strategy will be employed in order to deal with suicide or terrorism in general in regard to the fact that this is the gap that this article seeks to feel.

Several articles and research that has been carried out addressing different types of terrorism on suicide bombing. It has been noted that suicide terrorism is a strategic plan that in most cases have been considered to have a different government and political goals (Lennquist, 2012). It has been noted that it is done intentionally in order to make the government do or change some of the policies that are considered not good by the public opinion. The articles of study have considered terrorism is an organization factor other than being national government idea in order to cause fear among a target audience. Lennquist (2012) provides that Suicide terrorism has been identified as a form of expressing terrorism in different ways for example demonstrative terrorism and in a destructive terrorism. It is seen that suicide terrorism is a way of imposing hard pain to the part of the society that is opposing the interests of the terrorist's demands so as to cause the government listen to their demand or the other part of the society to join them in trying to seek for their demands (Lennquist 2012).

Suicide terrorism does not apply the same way the military force that is employed by the government to correct an error but rather suicide terrorism is used to lay down certain force that will make it easier for the government to easily realize the demands (Metzger, 2006). It has father been noted that suicide terrorism is made to reduce more damage than rather the states that face the military forces or economic sanctions. According to Metzger (2006), it has further been recorded that the current debate that is majorly noted to support the military forces is taking a wrong path despite its extensive use, it has done nothing in the stopping of the suicide bombing. The article suggests that homeland security and its own way of the defensive mechanism is the best solution to curb suicide terrorism. Despite the author's suggestion on this way of stopping terrorism suicide, there is no clear explanation on the way the method will be employed to handle the task in a way that this study seeks to real feel. It is well explained that any police department can become more effective at prevention without necessarily incurring a high cost simply by just increasing their education and becoming more observant on any abnormal acts that might happen in their communities. It is also explained that the police has the duty of educating themselves on how to deal with community issues using the modern way of dealing with such threats.

Terrorism is a very sensitive issue in the society that should be addressed with great concern while it has now been noted that the efforts of the government to contain terrorism outweigh the cost. It is recorded that the foreign terrorist who entered the US either as tourist or immigrants are the cause of around 90% of the deaths that were caused by terrorism. The government of the US has the responsibility to screen all the foreigners in the country especially those who are posing a threat to the nation in regard to terrorism and the health of the US people. It should be kept in mind that not all the foreigners born in the country are responsible for the terrorist attacks that take place in America and therefore, there is no good reason to flee all the immigrants from the country. It is well evident that terrorist have the ability to use explosives in the whole earth and clear records show that they will continue to use the same devices to inflict harm to the people of the country.

Very many departments in the US government, for example, the department of homeland security, in coordination with the department of defense and the department of justice has developed a common interest to combat the use of explosives by the terrorists. The situation in Israel where the mood of the country was changed by the intensified suicide bombing is not so different from what is happening in the US. Suicide is more of being effective and inexpensive, they are also regarded as being more complicated than any other form of terrorist that has ever been experienced. It is, therefore, referred to as an ultimate smart bomb. In order to clearly understand suicide terrorism over a group of people and the strategies, one can employ to counter the issue you are supposed to visit the people who have been affected deeply. Unlike those back days where you could easily note the terrorist since they just carried bombs in black polythene paper. You cannot easily recognize the nowadays terrorists nor the suicide bombers since these people involve both the married and the unmarried and both men and women which are more different from the past days where we only had men of young age being involved in such activities of terrorism. It has been discovered that terrorist is very much inventive and more of being flexible.

It is true to say that a person who is wearing a bomb is much more dangerous than a timed bomb that is left to explode in a place that many people are expected such as a marketplace. When the analyst try to weigh the cost that will be incurred when trying to save a single life under the proposal of the regulators on the ways that they can ensure safety it still remains a dilemma to the country since the cost mighty be too high to sustain the whole population of the US (Cordesman, Anthony, & Ahmed, 309).

Besides the fact that human is very expensive to compare with any kind of factor that can reduce the safety of the human life it is also not infinitely so. It is also said that Americans at a time try to do another thing that increases their chances of violent murder or death. Sometimes it is hard to reason the value between zero and infinity that some other individuals place their lives. The analysis also proves that when we have scarce resources in the country the level of terrorism is likely to reduce hence increasing the number of lives that are saved compared to the cost that is incurred to save the lives.

Back in 2010, the department of homeland security produced the actual number of lives that were saved in every terrorism that occurred using $6 million, then the value was multiplied by two to $12 million per live saved for unknown reasons. According to (Hahn, Lutter & Viscusi, 30), it is estimated that every effort that is made to save a statistical life is $15 million. Besides the cost that is incurred to eradicate terrorism there are other costs that should be inclusive of the terrorism cases this includes the damage cost, the cost used to care for the wounded and the economic disruptions. However, the costs are recorded very differently considering the three types of terrorism caused by foreigners. It has always been said that the cost of the lives that was lost in every terrorist attack is higher than the value of the economic and property that are damaged during the terrorist activities. The risk of terrorism can be understood in very many different ways for each visa category (Iapa News, 122). The following data records will give out a clear record of the number of deaths that might be caused in every foreign-born terrorist in a particular visa, the total number of foreign-born terrorist in every visa category the actual number of deaths that is caused by the foreign-born terrorist in every visa attack and the chances of the foreign-born terrorist getting a visa and the actual number of deaths that might be caused for every visa issued to the foreign-born.

If you multiply the total number of murder cases in every visa category by a total of $15 million per the victim will give the estimated value of the terrorism. The government of the US issued around 1.1

billion visas, of those the categories exploited 150 foreign-born terrorists that had entered the US from 1975 to 2015. Of the total number, some of them were granted, terrorists. In other ways, we can say that in every 7.5 billion people who entered the US only one person was recorded a foreign-born terrorist. As earlier noted that, 3,024 people were killed in the US by the attacks that were caused by the foreign-born terrorists in 1975 to 2015. The costs of the attacks were estimated to have laid a cost of $45 billion in the human life and that means the terrorist attacks cost equals to $39 per every visa issued over that period of time. It was recorded that the attack that was done back in the year 2001 September 11th also referred to as the 9/11 terrorist attacks were the deadliest in the word history. Therefore, excluding the terrorist attacks of 9/11, the cost of human life terrorism is lower to $600 million during that period of time. Of the total number of around 150 terrorists, it is recorded that around 110 of the terrorists did not murder anyone in a terrorist attack that occurred. Many of the terrorists had been arrested by the police department before they could execute their attacks or before their attacks could take any of the lives. Including those who killed and those who did not kill during the attacks for all the terrorism activities that occurred it is estimated that every terrorist killed around twenty people causing a total of human cost of $290 million. Although research that has been conducted by specialist show that, if not of the 9/11 attack each terrorist killed an average of 0.30 people per terrorist. On average it is recorded that only 39 of the estimated 150 foreign-born terrorists caused death to anyone. Of the 39 terrorists, each had killed an average of 75 people thus causing a damage of $1.1 billion worth of the human life. When the 9/11 is excluded the death caused by one terrorist reduces to less than two deaths per every terrorist and an average cost $29 million was the amount that inflicted by every successful terrorist.

Among other factors that are related to terrorism is the welcoming of the refugees into the country. A refugee is a person who has fled his/her on country maybe because of reasons of religion, race and political opinion. The refugees in the United States of America had to apply for a third country to be granted a visa before they were actually admitted in the United States of America. The refugees after a stay of one year in the United States of America, the law expected them to have applied for a green card. Research shows that of the 3.2 million refugees that were admitted to the United States of America from 1975 to 2015 only about 19 of them were terrorist, in other words, we can say that in every 162,000 refugees that were admitted in the US only one of them was a terrorist. Of the nineteen refugees who were discovered as a terrorist, there were only three who were successful in their attacks killing a maximum of three people. The analysis that has been going on for matters regarding suicide terrorism and the recent operations that were done in Iraq. It gave a large picture of how the military forces have always been the main target for the suicide terrorist, whether they are doing it directly or indirectly. It has always been stated that suicide has always been a response of foreign occupations. From the recent research that was conducted it was seen that the target for the military by the terrorist is mainly to make the military move out of the areas they actually consider their homeland. Some other studies have shown that suicide terrorism is at some instances organized as a military and political campaign. Regardless of how we will define the suicide terrorism, whether a target to kill the military is or if it is a politically motivated violence. Suicide terrorism is becoming a big threat to the US government and if it is not going to be given a big watch and control, it is likely to cause more harm to the people of the US. According to research, the US are likely to face the issue of terrorism even in the coming future. On the other hand, it is said that the elements of suicide terrorism will only succeed if the attackers kill themselves. However, in most cases, the success of the terrorist does not depend on whether he is going to die to live. This again remains the main challenge because the mission of terrorism must take place whether the terrorist will kill himself/herself or not.

## Review of USA Terroristic Threats

It has been discovered that the level of terrorism in the US reduced in the 1990s compared with the level of terrorism that was being experienced in the 1970s.

Terrorism remains a very sensitive factor that has affected the Americans in one way or the other. But the level of terrorism has been seen to be increasing steadily in the past around 6years. The incidents of terrorism were seen to be increasing from 1995 to 2000. The use of chemicals to destroy life by the terrorists, through the use of envelopes have been recorded to have caused the death of very many people in regard to using of anthrax (Sinclair, Samuel, & Daniel Antonius, 112). The FBI are still investigating any of the envelopes that are passing through all the postal office to validate this fact. While the terrorist incident that occurred in the 9/11 still remains a causality whereby a lot of people lost their lives in the incident. The terrorist act is posing more threats to the US as there is continued rise in the use of weapons of mass destruction. These have been recorded to go an increase since the attack of 9/11. The FBI reports have recorded threats of the cyber. The cyber threats range from juveniles to a group of people sponsored by the foreign powers. The theft of national security information and the interruption of the power using the cyber technology is a very sensitive issue to the security of the nation at large.

These might lay a lot of consequences if the issue is not given a better watch. Even the ones which are seen to be off list risk can lay a very serious threat to the nation in terms of the trading activities which are taking place in the country and the trade with outside countries. The fact that some people using the cyber technology can easily hack business credit cards that can cause a futile effect in regard to the trust of the consumers to the business because of the reduced security in their operation. This might reduce the consumer willingness to engage in e-commerce business with the affected country. Besides the criminal threats that are caused by the cyber, it can also cause a significant threat to the national security, this might include increasing threats from the terrorist attack from within the country and from outside the country. The terrorist is now using the modern technology to increase their funds, spread propaganda and might engage in other insecure communications that might cause a big threat to the national security more so if the information is misleading to the citizens of the US government. The use of the cyber by terrorists also referred to as cyber terrorism to close major government operations such as shutting down of power is a very serious threat that is emerging in the US. It was sometimes recorded by the FBI that the terrorists were trying to hack the US information system to obtain information of the water reservoirs, dams and nuclear and gas facilities. Although the FBI report shows that no such information as leaked out of the US system but the issue is posing a serious threat to the national security.

It is therefore very important to take very careful steps to prevent such incidences of national security in regard to suicide bombing and terrorist activity in the nation. Although the FBI and the national government of the US support the use of the modern technologies so that they remain competitive in the trading of the today global market. The technologies continue to pose a serious threat in regard to the national security. Misuse of the technology that has always prevented the US government from getting the required evidence to deal with the suspects of terrorism is also a serious problem to the

US government in their efforts to stop
terrorism and cases of suicide bombing. The
use of non-recoverable modes in the acts of
terrorism has been a serious problem since
the government is unable to get the required
information that has critical evidence over
the terrorists. The enforcement inability to
gain the very important information in the
required period of time has seriously
affected the ability of the government to
prosecute and prevent serious criminal acts
(Richman, Aaron, & Sharan, 175). The serious
challenge for the enforcement of the law has
created a big gap in national safety that
needs to be filled as soon as possible.
Unless the FBI will gather other more
improvised means to get the computer data
that may have been used by the terrorist
using improved electronic surveillance, then
the national security is heading in the
wrong direction and that our people are
likely to face the worst in the near future
on the matters of insecurity in regard to
suicide bombing and terrorist activities.
This is true because the investigator and
the people who are supposed to prosecute the
terrorists will be denied the very important
information that should be used to solve
terrorist activities and serious criminal

acts that are likely to happen in the near future.

## Suicide Bombings in the USA

The concept of self-sacrifice has been regarded as part of war in most instances and that people try to give out their lives in order to do harm to another country or their own country due to factors of political differences. According to the studies by scholars on the information about suicide bombing is that the concept was evident some hundred years ago. Therefore modern suicide bombing has been defined as a way used by the terrorist to destroy other countries using explosive deliberately. Sometimes it is claimed that it is not only the military or the political leaders who are the target but also the civilians to inflict pain on the nation. In the times of the civil war in Sri Lanka, suicide bombing was adopted as a tactic, and they practiced the tactic using bombs made of belts also referred to as belt bombs and they also used female bombers to accomplish their mission. Using the tactic of suicide bombing the people of Sri Lanka from 1987 to 2009 had killed around 980 people with their people committing around 80 suicide attacks. There have been several incidents of a suicide bombing in the USA and incidents of terrorism that have been experienced in a couple of years. The incidents of suicide bombing are not in any way expected to end soon since a lot of factors that are required to be put in place by the security personnel and the national government have not been adhered to yet.

In the year 2002, there was an attack that was done by two Muslims in the Maryland causing the death of ten people and serious injuries to 3 people. The pair had also been suspected to have caused other attacks in the Maryland. But according to results which were brought to the table after a short research was conducted, it showed that it was an affinity as a cause of the Islamic "jihad." Another incident of terrorism that has ever experienced is the attack in the USA is the letters that were being sent yet tainted with chemical substances. The incidents the main target was the political leaders and the government officials. The suicide that was committed by one of the biodefense known as Ivins created a series of questions to the FBI department (Thomas &

Irv, 250). The curiosity on why Ivins had to commit suicide led the intelligent department to carry out research in regard to the matter in question. It was thereafter they concluded that he had conducted suicide because he was guilty of the attacks that had involved the use of chemicals in the tainted letters. This is because Ivins helped in the creating of the chemical having targeted two of Catholic lawyers whom he thought were not conducting their judgment rightfully. However, some studies which were later conducted could not approve FBI report since there was no evidence in any of the letters that were linking this man with any mailing that caused the deaths that had occurred. Research of who is a suicide bomber and what motivates them has always raised several questions to every individual and most of them have always ended up with different conclusions. The fact that they always conclude that the suicide bombing is done by young people have failed to clearly elaborate or to give a stable set of records on the psychological, socioeconomic and demographic variables that can be linked with the suicide bombers. Another research that has been conducted recently describes suicide bombing not only being the jihadi factor but also for reasons of anger, pride and the feeling they are powerless. These factors have also been discovered to have a greater trigger to suicide bombing. In Texas back 2009 Hassan was recorded to have practiced an incident of suicide bombing after killing 13 people and causing serious wounds to 29 people saying that it was jihad to protect his fellow Muslims whom he thought they were being mistreated by the government of the US. A ruling of the death sentence was ruled against Hassan. A criminal justice professor argues that those people who practice suicide bombing are neither normal nor stable. He further says that these factors are driven by religious consequences (Lindquist & Sten, 90). Some of this people just want to die in a veneer of a heroic action. A study that was conducted showed that the remains of about 100 bombers showed that they had no complete body parts and others were suffering from dangerous diseases for example leprosy. The research further shows that the suicide bombing was done from the bottom up and not the vice versa, it was just a matter of following friends. Some of the terrorists are believed that they only crave for destruction just out of their bad moral reasoning and the beliefs that hold their deeds sacred.

## USA Suicide Bombing Attempts

There has been a lot of suicide bombing attempts that has been recorded to have been plotted against the United States of America since the start of the ninetieth century. There are very many terrorists who have been arrested as soon as they were discovered that they had an intention to cause destruction in part of the American states and parts of the American cities. An American young man was arrested after he was discovered to have been working together with terrorist and other studies proved that he was also providing material support to the terrorist. The American citizen who was changed in the court of law on matters that regarded terrorist was discovered to have the plot to commit murder in the country. The incidents were discovered and recorded back 2009. Another instance of suicide bombing attempt in the United States of America was discovered when a citizen from Morocco was arrested by the FBI police department after he was allegedly discovered that he wanted to carry out a suicide bombing in the United States of America's capital (Thomas & Irv, 44). The citizen from Morocco in western African was sentenced 30 years in prison. At the recent years, the intelligence organizations of the US has been working intelligently to make sure that that they prevent the plot against terrorism in the country. Their efforts have in many cases been seen to produce the best of the fruits.

The United States of America should operate under a very careful watch to prevent such incidents from taking place. Another person was found in Texas ready to perform a terrorist act. The police of Texas took the young man to the court of law where his case was ruled out and he was thereafter sentenced to life. Most of the suicide bombing attempts that in most cases get about to happen in the United States of America are found being done by mostly the foreigners. Some of the young boys and men have been discovered to be involved in the activities because of financial problems and some are involved just out of being curious. They want to experience what they see and hear from the media. Research that has been recently conducted show that in most attempts the people who are caught in the instances of attempting suicide terrorism and terrorism. Unless proper education is preached to the younger generation and they are guided and counseled properly on matters regarding the society, these youth are likely to cause more harm to both the United States of America and pose a threat to other countries if they continue with this rate of being idle and being too curious on, matters they don't know well about (Int'L & Business, 143). Unless the attempts and the incidents are given a great watch by the security department and the intelligence departments. The security of the country on matters of terrorism is at risk.

## The Analysis

Despite the focus on the terrorism factor that is being considered in the whole world. One main focus should mainly be on the threats that are facing the United States of America. The threats majorly include both the domestic and the international terrorism factors. While the discoveries that have been made recently show that domestic terrorist attacks have always been producing low causalities. The attack of 9/11 had the

worst damage that has ever been recorded in
the US. Terrorism has been regarded as a
continuing threat to the US government have
been causing a lot of deaths in the country.
It has been seen as a very serious challenge
to the US intelligence department who keep
on gathering information about the terrorist
attacks and the easiest ways that they can
easily get hold of the terrorists. In regard
to the threats that the terrorist activities
have caused to the government, the FBI have
formulated other more improvised ways to
deal with the issue of terrorism such as the
development of the broad-based
counterterrorism program to make sure that
they are able to get the information about
the terrorists and the terrorist activities
which they are most likely to perform. The
approach that has continuously been laid by
the FBI has always yielded a lot of success
on the security of the United States of
America. The flow of the terrorist threats
across the US need that better and more
improvised methods employed and continually
refined and adapted by all the intelligent
department and the security offices so as to
provide the most effective response to the
terrorist activities and make sure that the

citizens of the United States of America are living in a very secure environment.

.

# CHAPTER THREE

## Profile Befitting Suicide Terrorists

Suicide bombers are just criminals like the others since they tend to organize themselves so as to engage in ordinary crimes. These crimes may include robbery, theft, and drug trafficking. The crimes enable them to support and improve their criminal activities (Khosrokhavar, 2005). Their attack makes their lives sustainable. For these suicide bombers to perform their brutal acts, they follow some strategic steps. These steps include obtaining belts which are explosive and can be hidden in their bodies. They also choose target areas and come up with methods they would use to arrive at the spotted target. Lastly, they should have a plan on what to do before they reach the places of the target as well as the appropriate measures to take while at the place of attack. These steps are almost similar with those followed by criminals.

# Characteristics of USA Suicide Bombers

Most of the people who are involved in suicide bombing are intelligent, in that they have a specific level of education. About 32% of all the bombers have at least secondary education while 25% have a little of college education (Weinberg, Pedahzur & Canetti-Nisim, 2003). These people use these tactics to attack and bomb, thus resulting in the loss of a large number of lives. The majority of these bombers are kidnapped from this education background and then influenced to engage in the practice. They do this because of the benefits they are promised to enjoy once they get involved in suicide terrorism.

Those who are unmarried do not choose to remain in such situations, but it is only that they do not get the time or opportunity to marry since they are ever busy planning on several attacks. Many engage in a suicide bombing to get a political advantage or religious favor. In contrast, those who are married do not get a chance to visit their families due to their busy moments.

The majority of men involved in suicide bombing are between 17 to 23 years of age. Also, the old men and women are also recruited to fill the existing gaps. This helps in increasing the number of bombers, which improves the success of the act. More youths are involved since they have the required age which can bear the consequences experienced. Moreover, youths are encouraged to get involved in a terrorist attack since they are muscular and energetic, thus able to attack without cowardice (Kimhi & Even, 2004).

The majority of the bombers are from the Islamic community. This has been proven by several researchers who have conducted research. This can also be deduced to be true due to the kind of the terrorists who attack most of the institutions and states (Kimhi & Even, 2004). From the notorious Islamic terrorist, Osama bin Laden, it can be proven that the Islamic community is the main religion with the highest number of terrorists.

Lastly, the bombers have some months allocated for the indoctrination training (Weinberg, Pedahzur & Canetti-Nisim, 2003).

This period is very crucial to the new bombers since it is through this that they get equipped with the relevant skills of terrorism. After the training, the trainees are said to have graduated from one step to another, a state known as the hypnotic, where they can begin their mission.

## Martyrdom and the Culture of Death

In the fight against suicidal terrorism, martyrdom has been a major discussion since many of the bombers are believed to take this form of belief which is being associated with some religions. In its main agenda, it has been discussed and categorized into two forms. One is concerned about national agenda (Religion, 2011). In this case, some countries have been victims of the national agenda suicidal bombing. They include Palestine where people have been giving out their lives to save their country and its internal matters. Similarly, some other people do sacrifice their lives for transnational nature. Martyrdom, in this case, is devoted to giving their lives to Islamic community from all over the world with their main agenda being to destroy those are against their faith. Additionally, there is a culture of death that has been coming from a type of pilots known as Kamikaze, who have been a major point of many discussions in the modern day suicidal bombing (Khatib, Matar & Alshaer, 2014).

When a comparison of the suicidal bombing was made, it showed that it is possible to get a glimpse of how suicidal bombing has been evolving over time. Though not all pilots were willing to sacrifice their lives, it was obvious some of them are quite obliged to the matter of causing mass killing to innocent persons. The main thing is that these bombers are not willing, but they are just persuaded by their masters (Shahar, 2002). Therefore, with this regard, USA should be able to come up with awareness programs to enable its citizens and security officers to combat suicidal bombing. It is very worrying that some families in Palestine do volunteer their families for the suicidal bombing. This can only be eradicated by creating awareness to all people from across the globe on the value of life. If the USA takes such imperative measures, it will be in a position to safeguard both of its internal and external properties. According to Religion (2011),

USA comparison of strategies gives a valid and reliable solution on how to solve the problem of suicidal bombing as experienced from different countries and how they have been able to eliminate or reduce its impact.

Martyrdom has been known to be in existence in the war against the crime of suicidal bombing. Most of the reviewed literature have shown that Kamikaze pilots give a clear and a starting point of explaining operations carried out by Martyrdom. From Kamikaze's existing culture about suicidal bombing (Pierre, 2017), their culture is still taking place, and its effects are being experienced in Palestine community. Therefore, suicidal bombing mission, which is found within kamikaze pilots, has been used and still continues to be used as the primary reference point in our examination of today's suicidal bombing. In one of the Japanese cases, they implemented and adopted an ethical behavior known as bushido (Religion, 2011), which was used to mean a given way of war and owns voluntary means of death that has roots in their traditional beliefs. From as early as 18th century, bushido form of suicidal bombing has been a way of the warrior. Since

the existence of Japanese history, a war of
self-destruction has been on the move and
was mainly used as a form of avoiding one's
shame and a way of giving courage, honor,
and proof of personal integrity. According
to Drinkwine & Army War College (U.S.)
(2008), in Bushido teaching, values of honor
are taught in conjunction with obedience.
In light of these traditional teaching, USA
has to focus on how they are initiated on
individuals. After a successful
identification of how they are convinced to
have self-destruction, mission programs
towards eliminating the traditional vice
from the society has to be taken.

From the perspective of bushido teaching,
those who were obligated to serve did not
have a choice of selecting whether to take
part in the suicidal bombing or not. They
were to comply with the mission and dance to
the rhythm of the song. As Japanese, they
were believed to have a duty to die for
their patriotic act of the whole nation. The
same thing has been found in Palestine ways
of influencing people to carry out suicidal
bombing (Wicker, 2006). After Japanese and
Palestinians execute their mission and have
an opportunity to back out, they are branded

as heroes. In Palestine, these suicidal kamikaze pilot bombers are enshrined while Palestine places suicidal bombers on posters of Martyrdom. According to Palestine beliefs, they are very proud of giving out both their daughter and sons for suicidal missions. The big question is, should today's society be trapped by use of such simple lies? Individuals should be aware of the importance of life and shun such vices that entertain young people to register as suicidal bombing victims (Religion, 2011).

In all of the scenarios, martyrs are taken with high regard in their society, and consideration in such mission is of very high concern and all personal sins committed in one's life is cleansed. It is believed that Martyrdom death is fastest and a guarantee to the paradise where there are 72 virgins waiting for such brave people (Pierre, 2017). In regard to USA suicidal mission, it is worthy to take note of the techniques various countries believe, which are initiated to victims of the suicidal bombing. To save the USA from such teaching and avoid witnessing advanced effects, people should be educated on the lies and propaganda being spread to the victims. This will enable people to change their attitude towards suicidal bombing consequences. Target victims will shift their attention from such activities and realize the value of life. America will have to come up with a way of reducing risks that may be suffered through initiated suicidal bombing.

Finally, in most of the literature that has been reviewed, it has been confirmed vengeance integrated with human nature on humiliation plays a significant role in suicidal bombing activities. These are facts that have been collected from the ongoing conflict between Israel and Palestine (Shahar, 2002). Violence plays a major role in fueling suicidal bombing activities. Nevertheless, suicidal bombing in its nature has been associated with political mission accomplishment, but the end goal is the spirit of Martyrdom. Therefore, Martyrdom has been fueled by many other factors that make people get involved in self-sacrifice actions of being involved in the suicidal bombing. Promises that attract these victims to such missions are only geared towards achieving the set country goal. To eliminate the doom that Martyrdom brings in our society, USA should engage such countries that hold on such beliefs and try possible means of eliminating it. Close ties to military cooperation and other business related activities can help in eliminating the vice from the society. Religion (2011) postulates that it should involve religious leaders who are the main target in spreading the poor meaning of Martyrdom in order trap as many people as possible.

## Factors Involved in Becoming a Suicide Terrorist

Though it has been the quest for many researchers to come up with reasons associated with the suicidal bombing, it has been very difficult to find any conclusive one. To signify this, authors have differed on meaning and nature of what transpires suicidal bombing (Kulick, 2009). There is no major factor cause, but it is a combination of factors that make people involve in the suicidal bombing. It would be quite wrong to presume that suicidal bombers are either mentally ill or they are desperate in life. Research has shown that every person can become suicidal bomber when provided with good terms of convincing how it is beneficial. There are various reasons as to why different groups of people participate in these harmonious activities. Much research has been done while trying to unearth the main cause of the taking part in the suicidal bombing but none has come up with a solid evidence of the root cause (Bukay, 2017). The mainly discussed speculation revolve around psychological issues and personal crises, religion, poverty, and politically motivated issues. None of this can be said to be the main cause, but they are all integrated as a motivational force behind the scene of the suicidal bombing.

Though some cases have proved bombers were suffering from some form of mental illness, higher percentage depict soberness and willingness to participate without any psychological trauma, mental disability, or emotions. Therefore, from the analysis of many types of research, it has been noted that psychological problems do not contribute to suicide bombing activities. In its solution finding and implementation techniques (Bukay, 2017), USA should come out with a clear strategy of punishing suicide bombers who end up pretending to be mentally ill. Families should be advised to take care of their mentally ill relatives to keep them away from being recruited into harmful activities without their consent.

Besides many other cases that can be cited, state repression has been categorized as one of the main reasons causing many people to participate in the suicidal bombing. In some Israel cases (Espejo, 2009), very few of the bombers were not motivated by state repression. In one of the case studies, a 17-year-old Iyad al-Masri involved in suicide bombing with a motive of avenging for a brother and a cousin who were shot by soldiers from Israel. In yet another similar scenario, Hebah, who was 19-years-old, blows himself in revenge of what had happened to his brother in a demonstration against occupation in Israel. Hebah was seriously injured and spent more than 40 days in a state of coma (Wicker, 2006). Notably, many of the suicidal bombers were under the influence of state repression such as Israel action.

In a good case study, one Palestine blew himself in revenge of other members of the popular Front Liberation of Palestine after their assassination by forces from Israel.

Important to note is that the USA should take note of the motivation behind suicide bombers. Therefore, the enemy in a foreign country has to be fought bravely to avoid civilian harm in order to keep a good relationship between citizens and the peace restoring forces in a given country. Hence, suicide attackers would have no mission of participating in a suicide bombing.

In some instances, it has been like Palestine; it was found they mainly involved in suicidal bombing due to frustrations of withdrawing from core Islamic values. The fact of the matter is that, according to Waked (2006), religious suicide bombers have gone astray of the root theme of religion and they are exploring just selected versions and parts of their religious books. Due to these findings, the USA should embark mainly on research since it seems there is no root that can be connected to the suicidal bombing. This calls for serious research from across the globe to find the motivation behind mass killing through this method. Lack of main cause of suicidal bombing shows some parts of the study has not been intensively researched. The United States of America and mainly department concerned with security in conjunction with selected security officials should come up with well-researched findings that can help in combating crime.

## Benefits of Suicide Bombing

One of the main advantages of suicide terrorism is the inexpensiveness. The operation is relatively cheap, in that the materials and resources required to make the atomic bombs together with the belts used to attach them require little cost during the manufacturing process (Alvanou, 2008). As stated in the Al-Aqsa documents, the manufacture of explosive charge required only $150 during the suicide mission (Pedahzur, 2005). The process of making these bombs is said to be relatively cheap since locally available resources such as gunpowder and nails are very easy to acquire (Kruglansk, 2009). Due to the little cost of these materials, the entire cost of the bomb is relatively low.

There are no escape routes required during the bombing. This is because there's no need for the organizations to plan for the return of the bomber who has been sent to invade the bombing. As a result, the bomber has to plan himself or find other means of rescuing himself in case danger invades him during the bombing mission (Alvanou, 2008).

Suicide bombing causes mass casualties, in that the number of victims of the bombing tends to exceed the resources required to rescue them (Pedahzur, 2005). This is an advantage to the bombers since it favors them by promoting their mission. The purpose of the bombers is to cause death, and this leads to their success in their unlawful attack. This conveys the intended message to the public. This leads to creating media attention to citizens to keep on watching out in the case of any attack.

Once the bombing commences, it is always difficult to prevent. This is so because the police officers tend to lose the courage of trying to combat the scenario in fear of losing their lives (Kruglansk, 2009). Similarly, the type if bombs and grenades used are very powerful, hence create a lot of destruction and thus makes the situation very hard to prevent. This is a benefit to the bombers since their main aim is to make sure that they perform their attack perfectly to cause mass deaths.

Suicide bombing is a source of financial incentives to the bombers (Pedahzur, 2005). The terrorists who participate receive financial promotions after they succeed in their mission of killing. This enables them to raise their living standards as well as increase their morale in the terrorism. Moreover, there is a gain of political favors by the terrorists as soon as they succeed in the attack. The act encourages donations to the groups that are involved in the act. This makes the terrorists gain more supporters in their act. Due to this, there is a corresponding increase in their number, which makes their group very compelling. The other benefit that arises from this is the lack of the post-interrogation on the suicide bomber.

In one striking illustration, broadly detailed in the Israeli press, the main female Hamas suicide attacker, a young mother of two, was purportedly having an extramarital illicit relationship; murdering herself and a few Israelis was said to be the main way she could reclaim her name. A significant number of the individuals who were enticed to partake in these sorts of exercises were activated or, maybe, allured by experienced selection representatives gaining practical experience in this specialty. Enlistment has only included urging a person to give up for the affirmed prosperity of the group and the utilization of influence and control systems, yet not real pressure.

## Effects of Suicide Bombing

Suicide bombing creates fear to the public. Many of the people who are vulnerable to the attack tend to get frightened, and this makes them live without peace because they could be attacked and murdered anytime. Many institutions such as schools enter into trouble since fear disrupts their minds, thus leading to inadequate progress in the class work (Khosrokhavar, 2005).

Political change is also witnessed in the states which come up as a result of the suicide bombing. This change can occur in the political bodies of the countries where they come up with political measures which would enable them to prevent the future attack as well as ways of combating the act (Atran, 2003). This would include employing more experienced police officers as well as training them to be able to conquer the terrorists.

However, suicide bombing leads to withdrawal from territories, in that many groups of people who are members of a particular territory tend to run away from their country after witnessing the death of their comrades (Benmelech & Berrebi, 2007). This comes up due to their fear of being the next victims in case of another attack. This can happen since most of the suicide terrorism causes the death of the attacker as well as the citizens. The leaders of the territories give up since he might be seen responsible for the death of the citizens.

Lastly, suicide bombing can cause the wear down of the opposition. This is due to the strong defeat that faces the parties involved in the act (Benmelech & Berrebi, 2007). Similarly, the opposition groups tend to show their weakness, which makes them withdraw from the act to avoid being murdered.

# CHAPTER FOUR

## History of Attacks

America has been on the receiving end of several suicide terrorism attacks over time carried out by several groups and intended to achieve political and religious motives. As early as 1920, suicide attacks were being launched against America and American objects in foreign lands. In 1920, a TNT bomb planted in a horse-drawn wagon in New York exploded on Wall Street opposite the House of Morgan, killing thirty-five people and leaving hundred more injured. The crime, believed to have been perpetrated by Bolshevist or anarchist terrorist, was never solved.

The year 1983, suicide bombers tracks exploded near the United States military barracks in Beirut, killing two hundred and forty-one Marines.

It is, however, the September 11th attack that made the United States and the world realize how powerful suicide terrorism can be if and when properly employed. This terrorist attack saw four airplanes converted into bombs targeting specific buildings in the country. The first airliner traveling at a speed of hundreds of miles an hour with the fuel of over ten thousand gallons was flown into the north tower of the World Trade Center in Lower Manhattan (National Commission on Terrorist Attacks upon the United States, 2004). Minutes later, the second airliner flew into the south tower of the same building, and the Twin Tower collapsed less than ninety minutes later, burying glass, steel, and bodies under the debris. Minutes later, the third airliner plowed into the western face of the Pentagon with the fourth airliner, believed to have been aimed to slam either into the White House or the United States capitol, landing on a field in southern Pennsylvania after the intervention of passengers on board the plane (National Commission on Terrorist Attacks upon the United States, 2004). More than two thousand and six hundred people died at the Twin Tower, with one hundred and twenty-five more dying in the Pentagon (National Commission on Terrorist Attacks upon the United States, 2004). Investigations revealed that the attack had been carried out by young Arabs, nineteen in the number, who were members of an Islamic extremist group based in Afghanistan. These Arabs had been resident in America for over a year, with four of them being trained pilots. The other young men had a minimal education, with some lacking the ability to communicate in simple English. The young men had managed to carry out the attacks in groups of five or four members armed with knives, box cutters, and cans of Mace or pepper spray. They hijacked the planes and turned them into deadly missiles that resulted in mass casualties (National Commission on Terrorist Attacks upon the United States, 2004).

The attack was not a surprise to the country, bearing in mind the warnings given by Islamic extremist groups of their intentions to cause mass killings in America. As early as 1993, these extremists had tried and clearly shown their interest in bombing specific landmarks in the country with the aim of causing harm and killing a significant number of Americans (National Commission on Terrorist Attacks Upon the United States, 2004). In February 1993, there was an attempt to bring down the twin towers by use of a truck bomb by a group led by Ramzi Yousef, resulting in the death of six Americans and injuring thousands (National Commission on Terrorist Attacks Upon the United States, 2004). Other sides of intention to cause mass deaths in America include the attempts to blow up the Holland and Lincoln tunnels and other New York City landmarks which were thwarted by the arrest of the organizers of the attack, issuing of a self-styled fatwa by Osama bin Laden and four others declaring that it was God's decree that every Muslim should try his utmost to kill any American, military or civilian, anywhere in the world, because of American "occupation" of Islam's holy places and aggression against Muslims, the near simultaneous attacks by the Osama bin Laden led group, Al-Qaeda of the American embassies in Kenya and Tanzania killing two hundred and twenty-four people twelve of them Americans, and the Al-Qaeda attack in 2000 of the destroyer the USS Cole using a motorboat filled with explosives aimed at blowing a hole in the side of a destroyer which nearly sunk the destroyer (National Commission on Terrorist Attacks Upon the United States, 2004). From these and many other attacks, the United States government had received enough warning of the intentions of the Al-Qaeda group to kill Americans (National Commission on Terrorist Attacks upon the United States, 2004).

Al-Qaeda had been formed by Osama bin Laden, following the defeat of the United Soviet in the 1980s, who had moved to Afghanistan to take part in the jihad (National Commission on Terrorist Attacks upon the United States, 2004). Bin Laden recruited other players in the jihad to from the extremist group with the intention of taking the jihad to other places. In his mission to bring greatness back to people who consider themselves the victims of successive foreign masters, Bin Laden stressed grievances against the United States widely shared by Muslims, starting with the presence of United States troops in Saudi Arabia and the American foreign policy with regards to the Middle East. By the time the attacks on the twin towers and the Pentagon were carried out, Al-Qaeda was an organization with the ability to recruit, train, and deploy these recruits against ambitious targets. The organization, by September 11th, 2001, was able to organize major operations in terms of evaluating, approving, and supervising the planning and direction of the operations (National Commission on Terrorist Attacks upon the United States, 2004). The organization had already carried out major attacks against the United States, starting with the bombing of the United States embassies in Kenya and Tanzania. The United States government under the leadership of President Clinton had tried to deal with the organization before this major attack. The government had launched missile strikes against Al-Qaeda targets in Afghanistan and Sudan in retaliation for the embassy bombings. The administration had also tried to use diplomatic pressure to have Bin Laden expelled from Afghanistan. Foreign agents paid by CIA were allowed to operate in Afghanistan to aid in the capture of Bin Laden and his chief lieutenants (National Commission on Terrorist Attacks upon the United States, 2004).

Research has shown that the group started training for the September 11th attack as early as 1999. Initially, the plan was to hijack ten planes and use them to attack separate targets on the east and western coast of the country simultaneously but was reduced to four planes due to the complexity involved in carrying out such an attack (National Commission on Terrorist Attacks upon the United States, 2004). New recruits were taken in to help with the carrying out of the operation, which was not initially members of al-Qaida but was Muslim extremists based in German. The United States government received chatter of the planned attack by Bin Laden, and in an attempt to address the expected attack, broke some Al-Qaeda cells, but the core of the organization remained unaffected. In January 2000, the intense intelligence effort glimpsed and then lost sight of two operatives destined for the "planes operation," the name given to the operation by the Al-Qaeda organization (National Commission on Terrorist Attacks upon the United States, 2004). The two operatives managed to get to California where they found a group of like-minded Muslims from different parts of the world. They also managed to live in San Diego openly under their real names without attracting attention to themselves. The operatives from Germany had arrived on the east coast of the United States by the summer of 2000 and had started their training to become pilots.

The fourth pilot moved to Arizona at the beginning of 2001 together with another operative and conducted his refresher pilot training (National Commission on Terrorist Attacks upon the United States, 2004).

When Al-Qaeda was preparing for the plane operation, the government of the United States was trying to get Osama bin Laden expelled from Afghanistan. The government renewed secret efforts with some of the Taliban's opponents—the Northern Alliance—to get enough intelligence to attack Bin Laden directly (National Commission on Terrorist Attacks upon the United States, 2004). This resulted in inconclusive evidence and sparked a debate on the involvement of the United States in Afghanistan's civil war. During the spring and summer of 2001, U.S. intelligence agencies received a stream of warnings that Al-Qaeda planned a major attack against the United States. Information presented to the president, President Bush, in August 2001 pointed to an attack against America overseas, resulting to several precautions being taken to protect American objects abroad. The Bush administration in its efforts to eliminate Al-Qaeda enlisted covert action programs in

Afghanistan and utilized diplomatic
strategies in Palestine and Afghanistan
(National Commission on Terrorist Attacks
upon the United States, 2004).

The plane operation planners encountered
several challenges that would have played to
the advantage of the American government in
preventing the attack if carefully
considered and if they were given any
importance by the intelligence agencies
involved in the fight against Al-Qaeda
(National Commission on Terrorist Attacks
upon the United States, 2004). One of the
intended pilots for the operation was
arrested for having to be in the country
illegally while undergoing his pilot
training in Minnesota. Zacharias Moussaoui,
the intended substitute pilot, had arrived
in the training and requested for a fast
track training on how to pilot a large
airliner but was arrested for being an
illegal immigrant. However, the officers
involved were unable to notice any
connection to Al-Qaeda National Commission
on Terrorist Attacks upon the United States,
2004). Other expected participants in the
operation dropped out while others were
unable to gain entry into the United States,

setting the plane operation back and creating a loophole that could have been exploited by law enforcement and intelligence services to learn of and take measures to prevent the attack. In August 2001, intelligence officers were able to track terrorists spotted in southern Asia to the United States but no urgent action was taken to locate them and arrest them, and no connection was made between these incidences and arrests to the impending major attack that the government was preparing for. The Al-Qaeda organization saw some disagreements in the summer of 2001 on whether the planned operation should be completed, with The Taliban's chief, Mullah Omar, opposing the attack on the United States but Osama bin Laden overruled him, and the other objections present within the group giving the plan a go ahead (National Commission on Terrorist Attacks Upon the United States, 2004).

On September 11th, 2001, eleven hijackers gained access to the four airliners through security checkpoints successfully without detention. They took over the four flights, taking advantage of air crews and cockpits that were not prepared for the contingency of a suicide hijacking. The hijackers went through the check in process in the different airports they used to board the respective planes, with several of them being flagged by the different agencies at the different airports contracted to man and run the security checks. Some were flagged for extra security checks for being suspicious due to the fact that they had no photo identification and could not speak any English. The luggage carried by some of these hijackers was also randomly selected for extra scrutiny, but nothing suspicious was found. Some of the hijackers were intercepted when they set off the metal detectors during the security check, but none of them raised enough suspicion to be denied access to the different airliners. The security officers, in the case of two of the hijackers who set the metal detector off, failed to resolve the issue causing the metal detector to go off.

The Federal Aviation Administration (FAA) and North American Aerospace Defense Command (NORAD), the agencies that the United States, on this day, expected to defend the American airspace, were unprepared to deal with this kind of attack which converted airliners into missiles. The NORAD did not receive a shoot-down authorization until twenty-eight minutes after the last airliner landed in Pennsylvania. The FAA Boston Air Traffic Control Center was aware that a plane under its control was being hijacked after a flight attendant in one of the aircraft made an emergency call that lasted over twenty-five minutes, giving an account of the hijacking process in one of the planes. Communications from flight attendants helped the agencies identify the hijackers by name based on their seat numbers. When the first and second planes were hijacked, the FAA did not notify other planes of the hijacking, and this is how the fourth plane was caught off track despite taking off twenty-five minutes after the other airliners had been hijacked. The FAA lacked the capacity to deal with multiple hijackings and were not even prepared for such an attack. They started speculations on planes that could be hijacked next and came up with wrong conclusions. They ordered for American airliners to be grounded, followed by an order to ground all united airlines. Aircraft were also advised to increase security around the cockpit, but this was a little late, for the four airliners had already been hijacked.

The response to the attacks on this day all faced the problem of command. The attack at the Pentagon was met with a lack of command and control, but the citizens in the building tried to save one another. The passengers in the fourth plane fought off the attackers, resulting in its landing in an open field and not the capitol building or the White House as was initially planned by the terrorists. The involvement of local law enforcement agencies at this point of the attack was minimal and restricted to phone calls received from citizens who had been informed of the hijackings by passengers on board the airliners as the attacks took place. In New York City, the Fire Department of New York, the New York Police Department, the Port Authority of New York and New Jersey, the building employees, and the occupants of the buildings did their best to cope with the effects of almost unimaginable events-unfolding furiously over 102 minutes. The departments lacked unified command system and lost personnel in the attempt to help rescue lives. There was inadequate communication among and between the agencies. This lack of cooperation can be blamed on the fact that before this incident, the department of defense was not involved in the fight against terrorism.

## Suicide Bombing Risks in USA

Experts have considered the US homeland a high likelihood of having a suicide attack in the very near future. There has been a lot of threat attacks in the USA, which are outlined below:

In Baltimore County, a man with his family committed suicide in September 1995 in his car which was packed with explosives (Atran, 2003). The man had lied to them that he was taking them for school shopping where he finally lured them. After the police investigations, they found that it was the man's intention to lure his family.

A shoe Bomber by the name Richard Reid ignited an explosive in December 2001.The explosive was in his shoe when he was in an airplane moving from Paris to Miami. The passengers and the flight crew tried to overwhelm him from the trouble, though he supplicated for being guilty of the crime—

where he acknowledged that he was associated with the Al-Qaeda (Asad, 2007).

A 52-year-old man who had a history of dealing with payments provided to support children as a legal battle was seen in June 2005 walking into the courthouse (Asad, 2007). The man had a grenade in his hand and strapped with a backpack in his chest as well. He was then shot dead two times by the police officers. After the investigation, this grenade was found non-functional.

In October, the same year, a student who had explosives in his backpack blew himself in the university football stadium at a place called Oklahoma (Asad, 2007). It was not precisely known whether he had evil intentions of killing his comrades, though a review which was made about his background uncovered many years of making bombs and explosives. It was also found that his property included large quantities of explosives.

In December 2005, a man who had run away from an airplane was shot dead by the Air Marshals of the Miami International Airport. It was said that the man was carrying a bomb while he was passing through the jetway, though his wife reported that her husband had a mental illness and he has denied taking his medication. The Air Marshals pled that they were trying to defend themselves by shooting the man so as to rescue their lives (Atran, 2003).

## Suicidal Bombing Future Trends

It is a reality suicidal bombers are at the top of their advanced stages of causing mass killing through suicidal bombing. Suicidal bombing has been successfully executed in countries like Iraq and Afghanistan (Morgenstern, 2009). They have been so destructive, and they have caused mass killing in these countries. It is worthy to note how it has shifted from being a local scenario in the USA and other countries to being a global menace. According to NATO Advanced Training Course on Future Trends and New Approaches in Defeating the Terrorism Threat, Gurbuz & IOS Press (2013), Al-Qaeda has gone extra mile to make suicidal terrorism a global phenomenon and it is believed to be one of the forces that is leading in causing mass killing through suicidal killing. With advanced methods being devised to counterterrorism, terrorist groups are coming with new techniques.

It has been speculated that in future, terrorism may end up possessing and using weapons which are capable of causing mass destruction such as making use of chemicals in initiating suicidal bombing (Attacks, 2017). It is known that Palestine may become suicide bombers by being close to chemicals such as cyanide. On the other hand, Hamas has managed using rat poison in manufacturing their bombs with the intention of poisoning main water supply in Israel. To tame technological use in terrorist activities (O 'Rourke, 2009), USA should make use of the advanced technology available to monitor all materials that are going around the web. It can solve this by setting up satellite capable collecting any information that seems to have extremist values in it. Information should be filtered and be screened to make it pure and free of use in only valid reasons.

Since 2003 Iraq insurgent invasion, the terrorist has relied on Improvised Explosive Device (IED) method to advance their mission on both USA and United Nation Security convoys. With these new inventions, it should be very worrying since future terrorist may come up with very sophisticated devices capable of causing mass destruction. Therefore, USA should focus on the main developments that suicidal bombers are making in order to counter their advancement.

# CHAPTER FIVE

## Local Law Enforcement Officers and Their Training

Local law enforcement officers and agencies in the United States refer to the police officers under the employment of local governments. According to Discover Policing, there are more than 17,000 state and local law enforcement agencies in the United States, ranging in size from one officer to more than 30,000. Local law enforcement officers include municipal, county, tribal, and regional police that derive authority from the local governing body that created it. The primary purpose is to uphold the laws of the jurisdiction, provide patrol, and investigate local crimes. County police officers operate in metropolitan counties and have countywide jurisdiction. Some counties have sheriff department which is tasked with handling minor issues such as security for the local courthouse and service of papers. The sheriff in other areas of different countries has more powers, particularly when no county police are available and are tasked with the enforcement of the law, exclusively acting as both sheriff and county police. County police can either be full service, limited service, or restricted services. Full-service county police department provides police services to the entire community irrespective of the different communities and may even be contracted to provide private security on a contractual basis to specific districts within the counties. Limited service county police departments provide security services to the unincorporated areas of the county and can provide police services to special districts too on contract. Restricted county police departments provide to county owned or operated facilities with the capacity to carry out road patrol duties and provide support to the municipal police departments within the county.

Municipal police departments range from one officer agencies, still referred to as town marshal, to the strong municipal departments like the New York City police departments with over 50,000 police officers. They mostly take the form of police departments in most towns and cities with the department size, budget, resources, and responsibilities depending on the town of the community being served. Metropolitan departments have jurisdiction covering several communities and municipalities like the Las Vegas metropolitan police department with its jurisdiction covering a large area coterminous with one or more cities or counties. Metropolitan police departments are normally mergers of several local police departments and local sheriff offices. The mergers are for the provision of centralized service delivery which ensures efficiency through the centralization of the command system and of resources specifically in communities experiencing rapid growth in population or in communities too small to afford police departments individually.

Local law enforcement agencies are granted specific powers that enable them to carry on their constitutional mandate. They are allowed to arrest and handcuff individuals whom they suspect of having committed serious crimes to be held in police stations or jail, pending their trial. They are allowed to carry out strip searches and cavity searches under specific situations. These agencies are tasked with the patrolling of the specific neighborhood with partners of a single officer tasked with the patrolling of specific areas.

## Staying Ahead of the Threat

In the process of USA government to eliminate threats associated with suicide bombing, some laws need to be enacted while strengthening the already existing ones. Laws are intended to put in place techniques that are meant to be adhered to regularly in the society. The enforcement strategy adopted should be a long term with its set objectives to increase the safety of the USA and its properties from across borders. The person in charge should be assigned the task for a long period of time in order to accumulate a lot of experience that would help in combating crime. The officer in charge should also be a resident of the area. The officer should be a member of the larger community targeting to increase security but not a member of the target group. In an ideal situation, the contacts to be involved in the law enforcement should be entrusted by the whole community by commitment and identification of within the same community. The reason of being entrusted with such a role by the community should be obvious that the personnel has grown up from the same area or their families and relatives are within the same community. The most important thing would be involving few but specific trained group whose members are either locals of the community or officers from state law security department. The state law security enforcement officers are mainly focused on learning and identifying specific cultures and other beliefs that would help in fostering community mutual understanding. They are still mandated to share both harmful and vital information that might be useful in solving the problem of suicide bombing.

The goals of using a combination of both security enforcement officers and locals are to bring together required and relevant expertise which would help in addressing uncertainties that exist between law enforcement and other groups that foster a lot of threat to the USA. This creates an effective collaboration with all relevant federal and other local agencies that are used to enforce security agencies that are operating from either within or outside its territory. Taking into account that it would be very difficult for Federal Bureau of Investigation (FBI) to establish such a long term required close ties with target communities, it may need to put in place another mechanism. These available options include local officers from FBI department contacting and holding both class and public discussion with community figures, religious leaders, and other willing community leaders (FBI Academy, Quantico & Virginia, 2002). This helps the USA in increasing and creating a high level of awareness within the community members. These academics are geared to offer FBI an opportunity to describe both of its roles and needs required by the community. This helps USA law enforcement officers and community have an integrated system that would help in thwarting suicidal bombing. While law enforcement officers are provided with an opportunity to address the society about risks and means of thwarting suicide bombing, they should also focus on seeking any desirable assistance that would help these officers gather required information to solve the problem at hand.

While securing the country from acts of
suicidal bombing, the contact law
enforcement officers should be adapted to
the cultural rules of the subject community
such as local greetings and social norms
that are valued by the community (Day, 2008).
Officers in charge should be trained on how
to differentiate various extremist cultures
from other religious groups. However, the
contact law enforcement officers should be
very keen and sensitive to religious groups
and other concepts that involve social
morals of the locals; they have to note that
members of the larger community should be
considered as normal American who are law
abiding citizens. They are to give relevant
signals to the officers on the security of
the country. Additionally, there should be
close coordination amongst the police and
FBI officers together with other social
agencies that not geared towards enforcing
laws of the country against terrorism. These
other local and social agencies include
(Pedahzur, 2005) all mental health agencies,
agencies concerned with child welfare, and
homelessness help group agencies. Though
they are not the major part of the law
enforcement groups, they should be

considered, and their views are factored
since there is part of a community which is
being targeted or targeting to execute the
erroneous events. By use of law enforcement
strategy, concerned officers have to
evaluate and identify any problem that might
be the cause of insecurity in the country.
The community can be used to perceive some
assumption like the members of the society
who might be highly affected and can be the
culprit. Further, law enforcement officers
and FBI should be ready and willing to
accept any mistakes and errors that are
likely to happen while they try to interact
with the large community members. This helps
create very acceptable and conducive
environment to gather intelligent
information through cordial interaction with
the society (Skaine, 2013).

When intelligent information is sought
from the community, some laid down
guidelines has to be followed in order to
remain within the boundaries of the
community beliefs and culture. According to
Skaine (2013), to seek any information from
the members of the community, law
enforcement officers should try as much as
possible to be open and transparent on what

they need from the general public. Similarly, the meaning of the laws in operation has to be defined by the local agents to make it more elaborate and clear. The changes that are imposed by the existing laws has to be addressed clearly and loud enough with immediate effect after changes are initiated. Are the laws geared toward alienating community members? If yes, to what extent? And if no, why should it be implemented in effect to the community? If information needs to be collected through interviews, it should be done in a natural ground where all members are free to participate in an open manner. Where respondents to give information are part of the extremist group, law enforcement agents need to make the process open and allow the community to select one of their members to represent them. In such a case, the volunteer and the information provided should not be seen or taken as an act of guiltiness. Moreover, according to Day (2008), law enforcement agents interacting with the community have to be in a position to distinguish rumors from the facts. The problems presented by the community has to be listened to by the law enforcement agents. This makes it possible to convince the community that the information being sought is geared towards solving their problems. Apart from addressing the act of terrorism, laws may provide these security agents with some projects to manage within the community in order to give them a good position to interact with the community effectively.

In cases where a certain group such as religion is associated with the terrorist acts, it is important for the government to take actions that can reduce the risks while combating crime. Some government officials, if not all, and media agents can be used to request the target group to be very proactive in some religious aspects and make the community understand the peaceful nature which is associated with the subject religion (Skaine, 2013). The good gospel about the peace associated with the religion should be used to end the terror acts from our society. Let all communities feel they are part of the large American community and continue to be a law abiding group full of development agendas. This was what transpired the 9/11 attack and community groups, as to feel they are worthy Americans. Law enforcement officers and programs have to be geared towards bringing people together and make them feel they are worth in their country. Finally, it has been proved how law enforcement, coupled with community victimization, can pose a great threat by various groups creating a solidarity in the name of fighting for their rights (Pedahzur, 2005). Law enforcement agents have to make sure these communities are factored while making key conclusions to make them feel they are part of the community. Therefore, America should use open technicality measure to make its agenda of fighting crime valid and not targeted towards a certain group or religion. This law enforcement technique is used to make sure some communities are not locked out of giving their participation regarding security measures of the community.

According to Connors (2005), fighting suicide bombing through creating and organizing local enforcement in the process of counter-terrorism police has to play a big role. With the view of what has been happening from across the globe, local policing authorities have to take a central part while putting all resources together in preventing crime occurrence. This takes a new strategy of putting available resources together, having a clear roadmap of operations, creating a diverse and multidisciplinary team and training involves personnel. When working with the diverse, integrated group to fight terrorism, it has been proved worth to work with since prevention mechanism are thought to be more effective when a well-coordinated and focused structure is created to work closely and smoothly to accomplish its set objectives. This tactic is thought to have been adopted by USA government after 9/11 attack (Pedahzur, 2005). The group put together should not be related at all; their diversity should serve to integrate ideas in order to come up with the tightly coupled team. From diverse ideas adopted in the group, various ideas make people have a different focus on the same idea, hence deep, and the highly sought decision is reached to fight crime. This structure is thought to have been formed in Florida and has produced effective results in some other areas. Currently, it is being implemented to be part of the strong and effective tool when fighting suicidal bombing terrorism. Some reasons have been highlighted as to why creating such integrated team is very crucial. It creates a very strong public control with a separate chain of commands, increasing attention when it comes to creating a unified strategic plan and increasing both efficient and effectiveness of collectiveness and emergency prevention response mechanism. A good case has been observed between law enforcement and Joint Task Force in the process of bringing interoperability within the military (FBI Academy, Quantico & Virginia, 2002).

According to Olson (2012), observation power as a counter-terrorism pillar can be implemented in the police and intelligence department. Being a large or a small group of security officers, this can be a more effective strategy with minimal expenses. To lower the cost of operations while achieving maximum effectiveness, education takes a central part by becoming intelligent, observant and pinpointing on suspicion indicators in the society. This methodology has been implemented in Israel which has developed a well- coordinated and effective national system to counter terrorism. In Israel only (Stork, 2002), more than 90% of terrorist target initiatives have been prevented through the use of this technique. Training should not be at a given point and instance in life. Israel has implemented this by creating awareness to its citizen by integrating this in the education system as early as from kindergarten. Citizens have been trained to be alert at all times on any suspicious packaging or warnings issued by the government. Through the use of this highly structured and integrated system from both the public and security officers, Israel has been able to thwart many of the planned attacks (Forest, 2007). Three techniques are highly used and relied upon by Israel; early interception of terrorism act, which mainly focuses on creating a well-coordinated system amongst the state and other local agencies. They should have defined means of sharing information from high-security officials to even the lowest level possible involved in maintaining the security of the country. With this focus, it will be wise to think of preventing terrorism even before it happens in order to avoid losses.

USA should focus more on training if winning the war against suicide bombing is something to be of the past (According to FBI Academy, Quantico & Virginia, 2002). Training has to take the form of well-

detailed instruction on different ways of
developing suspicion on individual who may
foster threat to the state. This makes it
very simple and easy to identify bombers
without having any misconception about the
intention of the bomber. Training should not
only focus on how to create suspicion but
also on possible means of confronting the
suicide bomber when identified. According to
Richman, Shapira & Sharan (2010), if the
bomber develops suspicion on the mission
about to take place and detonates before the
officers can intercept, highly specialized
means should be employed to approach the
scene. This should involve clearly defined
procedures that explain procedures developed,
clarified by the security forces and adopted
in other risk events while securing the
country. When a specialized officer
confronts suicide bomber, the officer should
be equipped with necessary technical skills
that may help in confronting the bomber in
order to prevent destruction. The officer
has to use specialized skills to counter the
bomber even without contacting any special
unit for assistance or to get further
instruction on the way forward. Training
offered has to be focused on specific and
crucial instructions regarding mental set

preparedness for unpredictable events that arise in undefined situations (Stork, 2002). Training has to be effective in order to give out the desirable outcome. After offering training, there is a need to carry out a continuous assessment on the officers to make them be ready and standby at any time. This helps in preparing them psychologically on the occurrence of suicidal bombing and countermeasures that are to be taken on such issues. Though training is very effective in many cases, it should not be only limited to elites and specialized groups. The Israel respondent was cautioning countries from focusing their training on elites only, while citing a sample case when an Israel doctor become suspicious of the patient who went to the hospital with a motive of executing a suicide bombing. The doctor, through the application of Israel training technique adopted by the government to enlighten all people, uncovered the terror and saved many lives. According to FBI Academy, Quantico & Virginia (2002), the program should involve all people since over-reliance on special units only may not give the USA desirable and effective results required in fighting crime. Israel advocates an integrated training from police officers patrolling on the streets, citizens who can save the country from awful events, to multi-equipped professional police. All these groups should have specialized training to meet demands of each group, but all of them should possess core competencies. Police officers in the street require very specialized skills compared to a senior officer at the office since the junior patrolling the street would be highly reliable on the spot fighting suicidal bomber (Stork, 2002). All groups involved in this new technical aspect of combating terrorism have to be aware of the premature detonation that mainly results from bomber being spotted by either police or citizens. In light of this information, it is very evident the USA has not developed a committed awareness on the ways through which they could identify and counter terrorism in advance. Therefore, USA has to make sure all people play an important role in fighting suicide bombing (Olson, 2012). It has to stop on pumping a lot of resources while training security agents only; it has to focus on public awareness too.

As laws to fight any form of terrorism are being enacted and the existing ones being amended to suit today's sophisticated terror group actions, some powers have to be delegated to the judicial system in order to grant them powers of executing the laws. Some of the suicide bombers are intercepted before detonating the bombs, and they are to go through a legal process, which is the mandate executed by courts only. Judges and magistrates too should be taught on how to interpret Congress laws and make an informed judgment regarding suicidal bombers and their supporters who facilitate these deadly events—this is because law enforcement and training regarding suicide bombing is a large integrated framework that needs to be well coordinated if it has to work effectively. Putting all security agents together, specialized developed units under Congress laws, public training on suicide bombing and judicial system has created a complex framework. Since this framework cannot thrive on self-drive mechanisms, there is need to establish a management unit that would focus on this newly developed framework. This makes it possible to manage all affairs raised by these parties while addressing the insecurity problem posted by suicidal bombing. Therefore, USA should focus on this framework if it has to counter

terrorism through the use of law enforcement
and offering training to its citizens. It
will help in making all USA citizens
vigilant when it comes to security measures.
It should borrow some of these
recommendations from countries like Israel
where they have worked very effectively. It
can help to avoid as many attacks as
possible as it has been observed from the
case of Israel.

Some United States police departments and
other security agencies have identified the
risk of future suicide bombers as imminent.
The units follow correct policies, undertake
training and are consistently evaluated and
improving their readiness. However, some
security departments have not yet taken the
issue of terrorism into their hands. They do
not see the threat as big and dangerous, and
they feel that their jurisdiction would not
point them. Police departments in the United
States are mostly dealing with increased
crime cases, and therefore they are putting
more effort, sacrifice, and resources to
these crimes.

Suicide bombing is an inexpensive and
effective method for causing mass killings.

These operations are less complicated, compromising, and easier to control by the terrorists than other operations that have been employed over time. Most of these suicide bombers pretend to be civilians to gain unrestricted access to civilian objects in order to commit these attacks and in so doing, commit deceit. Suicide bombing is more effective because it tears at the fabric that holds the society together. Most of the suicide bombers are learned people with much experience in bomb-making and other military operation. A big number of the people who are involved in suicide bombing are intelligent, in that they have a specific level of education. About 32% of all the bombers have at least secondary education while 25% have a little of a college education. Some of them are just local people and lack knowledge but forced to do so by various challenges. Due to lack of knowledge, most of them end up dead in the process. The experienced team includes pilots, doctors, teachers, and other professionals. They act and perform their operation in a professional way so as to get the police forces off-guard.

Anthony Davila

# Best Practices for Handling Suicide Terrorism

Countries such as Israel, Pakistan, and Lebanon have recruited police officers to enhance the eradication of suicide terrorism cases. The most important people in dealing with the issue of terrorists are the police officers, especially the defense forces. These forces can investigate the local terrorist menace as well as work hard to ensure vulnerable target protection of their jurisdiction. Most of the world's countries like Israel have very powerful police defense forces who can deal with any terrorist attack. Countries have realized the need to involve local police in counter-terrorism (Braton & Kelling, 2006). This has enhanced the prevention of suicide terrorism, thus creating peace in these countries.

Though best police efforts have been established, only a few crimes are followed by the arrest, and there is the need of coming up with a method of increasing this (Heaton, 2000). The offenders do not take the risk of severe punishment seriously since they think it is not easy to be caught.

Community policing is also another practice under the use of police forces. In this case, beat police officers have been assigned to specific neighborhoods to spend a given period of time with the residents by talking to them so that the residents can present the local problems they face as well as the troublesome individuals in their area. This has helped in reducing the issue of crime in such places. The community policing is also contributing in protecting immigrant communities from victimization by providing reassurance to them in these countries (Innes, 2004, Morris, 2006).

There is enforcement of drunk-driving laws in some of the agencies that are highly valued within countries jurisdiction, though other countries place a high value on the arrest of the narcotics. Crime proliferation in most of the local communities is influenced by this value. These law enforcement agencies enjoy organizational dynamics. The law enforcement agencies in the current culture are moving towards intelligence-led policing models rather than sacrificing their success in ancient crime-fighting activities that enhance terrorism fighting. There are continued education directives in the trends of law enforcement as well as increased local law enforcement levels of awareness in these countries which are promoting prevention of suicide terrorism.

These countries have introduced the provision of education to the youth. Countries have done this by making sure proper education is being provided to them by teaching them about the adverse effects of getting involved in suicide terrorism. Once they understand this, they will not develop an interest in terrorism. Many countries have devised this technique, and it is really helping the youth and the cases of terrorism have diminished. However, high levels of intelligence have also been exercised to the youth so as to abstain from certain groups of people who engage in unlawful acts.

Lastly, the governments of Israel are motivating the youth by providing jobs to them to prevent them from being idle. In the same vein, these governments are giving favorable salary to these workers so that they get the morale of putting more efforts rather than getting involved in illegal acts such as theft.

## State & Federal Emergency Responder Bomb Incident Training

## Various international violent
## Incidents

# CHAPTER SIX

## A Convincing Research

In the research, a number of reasons have caused an individual to become a terrorist. The combination of psychological problems and personal related issues have been cited to influence many suicidal terrorists to join suicidal bombing movements around the globe. These factors include religious, economic, political, and social. Any action taken to restore peace should be guided by ethical behavior that upholds human dignity. The act of respecting human rights greatly helps in building co-existence between nations. Therefore, the enemy in a foreign country has to be fought bravely to avoid civilian harm in order to keep a good relationship between citizens and the peace restoring forces in a given state.

Terrorists have greatly advanced in their knowledge of the military counter attack. Studies show that almost 10% of Muslims in America believe that suicide bombing on the defense of Islam is acceptable. Terrorism has gone to higher standards were suicide bombers plan a big project that takes around ten years and above but successively kills thousands of people.

The United States should always have a ready response plan in place in the event of terrorist attack. The plan should consist of ready security backup in targeted places. The high number of intelligence in the airport, big hotel, and another terrorist target will help to counter the terrorist danger. The United States has also come up with ways to fight the terrorist indirectly. These were done by educating the citizen on matters concerning terrorist. They are taught what to do when any kind of attack happens. They are also educated to keep security guard of themselves and report any suspicious act. Youths are given special education which helps them avoid radicalization. Through education, youths learn the negative effects of terrorism. Hence they disassociate from those groups. The culture of loving one another and value of patriotism is developed in the youths. The United States of America has come up with the anti-terrorism group. Operations need an early response from the Anti-terrorism unit. For example, agencies which, prior to the attack, operated independently. The federal bureau of investigation established the national security branch centered on fighting terrorism. These resulted in the decision that matters concerning terrorism was left to the federal bureau of investigations. Each department was assigned a specific role. The exercise of identifying and stopping suicide bombing requires effort by all units.

Building good relationship between nations, especially Islamic nations. This helps to create co-existence between nations. Sanctions are given to countries that are operating with terrorist groups. Making of a terrorist most wanted list can greatly help. The United States, in giving sanctions, makes those nations to understand the importance of peace and cooperation. Implementation of human rights can also help to reduce the heat on terrorist. Children are less expected to make such deadly attacks, so, mostly, security forces are taken unawares. It is becoming so difficult for a terrorist to stop such attacks, as death is the most powerful weapon of the terrorist. By receiving such support, terrorist can kill many innocent civilians. The United States has to control the use of nuclear technology. The United State of America can work in hand with private security and businesses to obtain secret, confidential information on this terrorist. Bank and money-transfer stations such as the Western Union can give correct details about suspicious money looting transfers; vehicle hire agencies, hotel room's rentals, and real estate agents can give you information about newcomers and can help to inform about bosses funding terrorist.

Suicide bombing and terrorism have affected the whole world. Suicide bombers force us to live with fear. All through my studies in this project, I had to use various sources to cover the topic on terrorist bombing. The research methodology was necessary because it involves the use of different resources. However, the research will be a comparative study which will pick the best practices across the world countries such as Israel, Pakistan, Afghanistan, and Lebanon and then identify actions taken by these countries to make their law enforcement agencies more capable of dealing with the suicide terrorism to prevent and combat the act. The two groups are: domestic and international terrorists.

Domestic terrorism refers to unaccepted threat using terrorist groups that are functional in the United States or any other country in the absence of any interference. This is done to property or a person to fraud a government or citizen. It is done for either social, political, or religious reason. International terrorism includes very dangerous activities and violent acts against the citizen, which are against human right and the constitution of the United States or another country. It can also be a criminal activity but done to pass a message to the United States or any country. These activities are purposed to arouse anger to the citizen, influence the political system of a government, or corrupt the system of a ruling party. These terrorists expand their activities across national boundaries in order to achieve their mission. These terrorists make target attacks which are accomplished within a specific time and place.

Terrorism is an act done by several groups, each having their own mission. They sometimes want to pass a message. Terrorists cause undesirable and adverse psychological impact; terrorist groups are the most dangerous threat to civilization. Their malicious will, coupled with their evil understanding on religion and politics, drives them beyond the sense of humanness. Terrorist bombers execute their actions at the peak of losing their life. All their activities are run by wealthy people who want to hit on a certain government or country. They pay a large sum of money to the terrorist groups, and these groups finally do the bombing. The terrorist groups mainly use young people to execute their mission. Terrorists use youngsters by using fake identification cards, having girls' photos on profile pictures through which they lure these youngsters to join them, use religious mishaps—giving them bad examples. In addition to trapping these youngsters by showing them girls' pictures, terrorists offer promises of money and cars, eatable items and food. Some youths run to these terrorist groups to look for protection. They are given knowledge as soldiers and later given explosives and guns.

Terrorist bombing is a long-term process. It can take a day week month or even years. A child is born, educated, trained to join military forces only to become the most wanted terrorist eventually. Many examples in the likes of Osama bin Laden have confirmed this theory. This strategy helps them to have full information about their target so as to choose a suitable method to carry out their attack. Terrorist groups using this strategy learn about security system of that country and mostly note its weakness. This gives terrorist confidence, as they have all the information they need. A terrorist has the day, time, and strategy to quit if the mission failed. Group countries such as Afghanistan and Pakistan are under serious military threat. Al-Qaida's authority is diminishing, thereby expanding its problem when trying to increase capital. However, the consequences of core leadership are making the issues of terrorism to increase in the border areas of Al-Qaida.

United State has set up special units to investigate and get information leading to arrest of such terrorist. This is called Anti-terrorist unit. Special Operations

Forces (SOF) have always held a certain important role. They often work unnoticed, living in the shadows of security files only. The Anti-terrorist unit is mostly made up of these specially-selected, highly-trained troops. Members of this group have all undergone military training. This special unit helped in the 1980s to stop attack threats in Iraq and Lebanon. This special unit effort was recognized by most elite members, accompanied by federal bureau units and Operation Eagle Claws, which later fought against Iraq in 1980. This agency was given a duty of counterterrorism activities in the maritime environments. Richard Marcinko was made the first commander. He once said that with only 75 shooters, it's unbelievable that unit had more fighting experience than all Marine Corps. America's spies have relatively done a good job. They helped Eagle Claw to identify the terrorist and know the possible target places.

Most suicide bombers are motivated by the attacks in Afghanistan, Iraq, and Syria. Terrorist organizations have greatly increased due to many radicalization activities with the aim of suicide bombing. Suicide bombing is the most dangerous form of terrorism, for it undertakes its obligation without loss of support from the terrorist groups. They are trigged by different reasons. Social motives are also linked to individuals' standards; broken families cause children to give in to the temptation of joining these societies. Such circumstances are usually accompanied by the lack of basic needs, thereby promoting rotten behaviors, and thus leading to the exploitation of the vulnerable/affected people by the terrorists. The terrorists assist these youths by providing for their needs, helping them overcome their challenges, and by this, the youth easily get interested in the terrorist activities, and thus young people are easily swayed.

## Weapon Used and Target

In the countries where the research was done, the different government databases on suicidal bombing were handled differently due to the difference in cultural beliefs. In countries like Lebanon and Syria, the application of rules against suicidal bombing proved to be somewhat lenient to criminals. If similar laws would be implemented in the USA (Waked, 2006), such criminals should be treated mercilessly in order to act as sample lessons to others. In other countries, these nefarious activities have been going without any law enforcement since it is a common belief that the criminal died and there's no way they could be brought back. In actual sense, there is no common pattern that suicidal bombers prefer in targeting; neither is their choice of weapons. The type of weapon used in a given situation is usually set to match with the proposed destruction plotted by the terrorist group. Though the nature of the weapon to use may be available, some other factors such as security of the place (Skaine, 2013), availability of the weapon, resources required to plan the execution of the intended terrorist act, and the expertise required has to be factored. For the USA to be able to control any form of a suicide attack, it has to put under control all weapons that can be used to launch an attack. Areas prone to attacks have to be given extra security measures to make sure they are very difficult to access. This ensures that all areas are secure and cannot be used as avenues for launching sophisticated attacks like the 2001 attack which brought a lot of destruction and left many of the citizens injured.

In addition, according to Rakhra (2008), women have been enlisted in the group, and they are being used to carry out many of the attacks that have been happening around the world. This has been evidenced in Pakistan and Russia. From the analysis, the USA should take bold steps in sensitizing its citizens on the possible means through which suicidal bombers are coming in to cause mass casualties. In terms of economic development, the major economic drivers have been the target of suicidal bombers, with the only intention of causing an economic crisis in a given country.

## Has it Sunk in Yet?

Death has been the most powerful weapon used by suicide bombers, which has made it very difficult for police forces to stop them. This method of terrorism has been used for demonstrative purposes and can also be limited to targeted attacks. The terrorists are mostly flexible and creative. A person with a bomb on their body cannot defend themselves.

The suicide bombers aim is to kill the largest numbers without discrimination, which helps the terrorists, and there is no destruction on the side of the terrorists. The Islamic concept of jihad has been used by most groups to explain their reason for suicide terrorism. Most of the Islamic theorists believe the real meaning of jihad in a military way—as a physical warfare—while some western scholars say it is an internal conflict. Terrorists have specific target places like airports, bus station, rail station, supermarkets, and big social halls.

## Recommendations

Pellegrini and Connors have written on how to encounter terrorism in the united nation soil. This involves the creation of local agencies, as they work in guarding and defending the country against external attacks. Most strategies aimed at encountering terrorism involve an increase in the standard of police and domestic intelligence. The basic activities are traditional: communication trapping and the identifying of persons. New technics have, however, expanded in terms of policing operations and weapons.

The United States had to form different ant-terrorism organization agencies. These agencies enhanced the member state capacity. The United States should also offer training to the youth, and especially her citizens, on ways to identify and counter terrorism activities. The United States has to develop a new method of knowing her citizens—through the immigration policing department. Foreigners have to produce legitimate visa, which gives valid reasons for acquiring the visa. The use of scanning machines and cameras can help the police forces—this includes CCTV working 24 hours. Terrorist mostly know that they are being watched, hence the United States should be ahead of them. Advanced machines are needed to counter suicide bombers.

The United States police forces should take threats and warnings given by these terrorist groups very seriously. Intelligent agencies should be able to provide sufficient information required to thwart terrorist activities. The law enforcement agencies in the current culture ought to move towards intelligence-led policing models rather than sacrificing their success in ancient crime-fighting activities that enhance terrorism fighting. The information gathered from government agencies would be used as primary information; additionally, it would be much relied upon when addressing terrorist problems and any challenge that had been faced when addressing suicidal bombing problems. In the research, other sources of information which were highly relied upon were publications written by other scholars, not only in the USA but from across the globe. Other materials which may act as a secondary source of information were factored in this research. The information collected from different sources was verified to make sure it matches the required standards in making a conclusive decision about the security concerns. There are government databases that contain very sensitive information; the data from government sources were considered to be very crucial and confidential.

Quick response from the Ant-terrorism unit is also vital for the operations of other agencies to be effective. For example, agencies which, prior to the attack, operated independently. The federal bureau of investigation established the national security branch centered on fighting terrorism, which resulted in the decision that matters concerning terrorism was left to the federal bureau of investigations—and here, each department was assigned a specific role. The United States can also try as much as possible to have a friendly relationship with other countries. In solving, conflicts between nations, diplomacy system can be used. This helps to soften the interrelationship between those nations and the United States. The United States should leave conflicts in other nation to the united nation organization, as this body helps to solve the conflict without favoring any nation—this is because it comprises members from almost all nations of the world.

The United States has to try to destroy all links of weapon supply to terrorist groups. Strict laws should be implemented to punish the weapon suppliers and to make sure all efforts to manufacture atomic and nuclear bombs are thwarted. Nuclear energy is the most reliable energy source that can constantly produce power. It is powerful than the wind, hydroelectric, solar, and safer compared to oil refineries—due to the minimal death rate and what the media says about it.

Before now, the Nuclear Regulatory Commission was not functional, and their duty was not to the standards that the society would have had something to do with. However, in the present time, the Antinuclear Commission has made a great effort in the nuclear industry by putting in place heavy rules on plants currently in use, and even tighter rules for the new plants that are set to commence operation.

The United States should give great sanctions as well as come up with a terrorist most wanted list, as these can greatly help. The United States should give both business and charity sanctions to those countries supporting terrorist groups. The list of most wanted terrorist will help develop unity policing against enemies. Respect for human rights should be established, i.e., by advocating the implementation of human rights. This helps those terrorist groups to feel considered and counted in the society.

The United States has to educate its citizen on the bad impact of terrorism and make them understand that the security and peace of the nation is on their hands. No one can maintain peace for the entire nation. Hence, everyone should take responsibility for his or her security. This will help to make the society aware of any suspicious acts and alert the relevant authorities or act if necessary. Through educating the citizen, the value of nationalism is developed. Nationalism helps to develop a self-governing individual, including the right identity and social position. This value helps United State citizens to love, trust, be loyal to their nation, and believe in the ruling government. It is the only value that scares terrorists away. The main thing is that these bombers are unwilling, but their masters just persuade them. Therefore, in view of this, the USA should come up with awareness programs to enable its citizens and security officers to combat suicidal bombing. It is very worrying that some families in Palestine do volunteer their families for the suicidal bombing. This can only be eradicated by creating awareness to all people from across the globe on the value of life.

Terrorism should be studied at all level, starting from junior classes. General knowledge of terrorism and the effect of terrorist should be well known. A citizen should know that there is no benefit of terrorism to the society. The expertise enforcement of laws in the government of USA should prevent severe attacks. This concern should be predicted in a watchful manner to identify emerging changes. The Federal Bureau of Investigation should be friendly to the citizens and use data given by citizen wisely.

The United States, with the help of other nations, should regulate media use. Media include Television, newspaper, radio, and internet. Terrorists mostly use the freedom of expression of the internet and media to threaten, fight, and give bombing alerts to the citizen. In the United State of America, the July 2009 report document established findings by the Federal Bureau of Investigation estimated that there were at least 5,000 websites and web groups that support terrorist acts, with around 10,000 of them actively maintained. Roughly 80% of these sites are being run on United States based Server. The United States should come up with inclusive vision and ideas for her people. This will help in countering violent extremist propaganda from terrorist groups. Terrorists use these ideologies to radicalize and recruit young individuals. Vision and positive, promising goals given by the government will help citizen to have trust and hope in their nation.

Development of patriotism by United State government is also paramount. Securing American communities from terrorist groups cannot be a work of the security agencies alone but all individuals. Groups such as Al-Qaida need civilian watch-out. The effort of citizens and the communities, especially Muslim citizen, are being targeted for radicalizing by this terrorist groups. The Muslim community can successfully help the security forces to in countering the bombers. Muslim American communities have been on the front line to fight against terrorist groups; they have been providing terrorist secrets leading to attacks. This community has also given insights on the recruitment of youth by al-Qaida's and other groups. One's loyalty to their nation matters a lot. A citizen should be able to stand for their nation. The act of nationalism makes a citizen do what is right for their country. Nationalists love their nation and are ready to die for it. Nationalists are happy when their nation is successful. Nationalism makes one have a good code of conduct, develop a spirit of love, unity, and brotherhood among other people.

# CHAPTER SEVEN

## Non-Law Enforcement Community Reviews

## Suicide Bombers—people that are Suicidal

In spite of expansion in the treatment of Suicide bombers over the previous decade, rates of Suicide bombing conduct have remained, to a great extent, unaltered (Kroenig & Pavel, 2012). Most epidemiologic researches on Suicide bombing conduct have concentrated on examples and associates of pervasiveness. The up and coming era of studies must look at synergistic impacts among modifiable risk and defensive components. New reviews must join late advances in overview techniques and clinical evaluation. Results ought to be utilized as a part of continuous endeavors to diminish the huge death toll brought about by the conduct of Suicide bombing. Suicide is a huge general medical issue in the United States and around the globe. Every year, more than 30,000 individuals in the United States and roughly 1 million individuals overall pass on by suicide, making it one of the main sources of death (Dahl, 2011). A current report from the Institute of Medicine (National Academy of Sciences) assessed that in the United States, the estimation of lost profitability because of suicide is $11.8 billion every year.

## Suicide Bombers as Viewed by the Medical Comunity

Reports from the World Health Organization (WHO) show that suicide represents the biggest share of the deliberate harm trouble in nations and that suicide is anticipated to wind up plainly a much more noteworthy supporter of the worldwide weight of illness over the coming decades. The reality and extent of suicide has driven both the WHO and the US government to require a development of information accumulation on the predominance of and risk variables for suicide and nonfatal Suicide bombing conduct to help in the arranging of general health procedures and social insurance strategies and in the observing of behavioral reactions to approach changes and counteractive action endeavors (Lankford, 2013). Tending to these calls, in this paper, we give a survey of the study of disease transmission of Suicide bombing conduct and amplify prior audits around there in two essential ways. To begin with, we give a report on the commonness of Suicide bombing conduct over the previous decade.

This announcement refreshes the past statement by the American Academy of Pediatrics and helps the pediatrician in the ID and administration of the immature at risk for suicide. The degree to which pediatricians give fitting consideration to young suicide bombers relies upon their insight, expertise, comfort with the theme, and prepared access to suitable group assets. All young people with Suicide bombing side effects ought to realize that their supplications for help are heard and that pediatricians will fill in as backers to help settle the emergency. The number of youthful killings from suicide in the United States has expanded drastically over the last couple of decades. In 1997, there were 4186 suicides among individuals 15 to 24 years of age, 1802 suicides among those 15 to 19 years old, and 2384 among those 20 to 24 years old (Dahl, 2011). In 1997, 13% of all killings in the 15-through 24-year-seniority group were inferable from suicide.1 The genuine number of killings from suicide really might be higher, on the grounds that some of these killings are recorded as "incidental." From 1950 to 1990, the suicide rate for youths in the 15-to 19-year-old group expanded by 300%.

## Infectious Virus Contamination Caused by Suicide Bombers

Suicide bombing conduct is the leading cause of damage and demise around the world. Data about the study of disease transmission of such conduct is vital for approach making and avoidance. The authors surveyed government information on Suicide and Suicide bombing conduct and directed a methodical audit of studies on the study of disease transmission of suicide distributed from 1997 to 2007 (Bergen, Hoffman & Tiedemann, 2011). The authors' points were to inspect the predominance of patterns, chance and defensive components in Suicide bombing conduct in the United States and cross-broadly. The information uncovered noteworthy cross-national inconsistency in the pervasiveness of Suicide bombing conduct, taking into account the consistency in a period of onset, move probabilities, and key risk variables. Suicide is more predominant among men, though nonfatal Suicide bombing practices are more common among ladies and people who are youthful, are unmarried, or have a psychiatric issue.

## Financial and Social Variables

The financial and social variables with which Suicide bombing conduct is related, for example, the quality and amount of emotional wellness administrations, have changed significantly, making it essential to look at whether and how the predominance of Suicide bombing conduct has changed after some time. Second, earlier surveys have concentrated on a particular nation (e.g., the United States), subgroup (e.g., young people), or conduct (e.g., suicide endeavors) (Clapper, 2013). We survey information from various nations, on all age groups, and on different types of Suicide bombing conduct, giving a far-reaching photo of the study of disease transmission of Suicide bombing conduct. In addition, given late technological advancements in harm reconnaissance frameworks, and the current finish of a few huge scales epidemiology, a review looking at the cross-national predominance of Suicide bombing conduct, a refreshed survey of this theme, is particularly justified right now (Sage, 2011).

In the United States, suicide happens at a rate of 10.8 for every 100,000 people; it is the eleventh driving reason for death and records 1.4 percent of all US killings. A more point by point examination of the information by sex, age, and race/ethnicity uncovers noteworthy socio-demographic variety in the suicide rate (Pham, 2012). There are no group contrasts until mid-youthfulness (ages 15-19 years), at which time the rate among guys' increments significantly with respect to the rate among females. The ascent for guys is most prominent among Native Americans/Alaskan Natives, expanding more than fivefold amid immaturity and youthful adulthood, from 9.1 for every 100,000 (ages 10-14 years) to 51.9 for each 100,000 (ages 20-24 years). The rate for Native American/Alaskan Native guys decays amid center adulthood before topping again amid more seasoned age. Non-Hispanic White guys likewise have a sharp increment amid immaturity and youthful adulthood (from

2.0/100,000 at ages 10-14 years to
23.0/100,000 at ages 20-24 years) and an
increment from ages 65-69 years
(23.9/100,000) to age 85 years or more
(49.7/100,000) (Bergen, Hoffman & Tiedemann,
2011).

The rates for ladies are lower and
basically not overlapping with those of men,
with two particular cases being suicide
among Native American/Alaskan Native ladies
amid pre-adulthood (ages 10-19 years) and
suicide for White unmarried middle-age
ladies (ages 55-59 years). Suicide rates for
individuals of Hispanic and Asian
race/ethnicity, not included in figure 1 due
to space requirements, were generally like
those for Black guys and females. A large
number of youngsters consistently submit to
suicidal tendencies. Suicide is the third
driving reason for the death of individuals
between the ages of 15 and 24. It is the
second driving reason for death among
students. As adolescents, it is difficult to
manage the enthusiastic and physical changes
we experience, and grown-up direction is
vital to help us through these circumstances.
Many individuals consider finishing their
lives; however, most don't end up doing it.

Suicide is the third driving reason for death for young people 15 to 19 years of age. Pediatricians can help forestall pre-adult suicide by knowing the side effects of wretchedness and other pre-suicidal conduct (Kroenig & Pavel, 2012).

Adolescent guys 15 to 19 years of age had a rate 6 times more prominent than the rate for females. The proportion of endeavored suicides to finished suicides among young people is evaluated to be 50:1 to 100:1, and the occurrence of unsuccessful suicide endeavors is higher among females than among guys. Suicide influences youngsters from all races and financial groups; albeit a few groups appear to have higher rates than others. Local American guys have the most elevated suicide rate, African American ladies the least (Lankford, 2013). A statewide review of students in evaluations 7 through 12 found that 28.1% of promiscuous and gay person guys and 20.5% of androgynous and gay person females had revealed endeavoring suicide. The National Youth Risk Behavior Survey of students in evaluations 9 through 12 showed that almost one-fourth (24.1%) of students had genuinely considered endeavoring suicide amid the 12 months going before the review, 17.7% had made a particular arrangement, and 8.7% had made an endeavor (Clapper, 2013). Guns, utilized as a part of >67% of suicides, are the main source of death for guys and females who confer suicide.8 More than 90% of suicide endeavors including a gun are lethal on the grounds that there is no minimal shot for safeguard.

Guns in the home, paying little mind to whether they are kept emptied or amassed up, are related to a higher risk of youthful suicide. Guardians must be cautioned about the lethality of guns in the home and be prompted unequivocally to expel them from the premises. Ingestion of pills is the most widely recognized strategy among youths who endeavor suicide. Albeit, no particular tests are equipped for recognizing Suicide bombers; particular risk components exist (Pham, 2012). Young people at higher risk regularly have a past filled with misery, a recent suicide endeavor, a family history of psychiatric issue (particularly melancholy and Suicide bombing conduct), family disturbance, and certain endless or crippling physical issue or psychiatric illness. Alcohol utilization and liquor addictions demonstrate a high risk of suicide. Liquor utilize has been related with half of the suicides. Living out of the home (in a restorative office or group home) and a background marked by physical or sexual manhandle are extra figures all the more normally discovered in youths who display Suicide bombing conduct (Sage, 2011).

## Additional Social Variables to Consider

Psychosocial issues and stresses, for example, clashes with guardians, separation of a relationship, school challenges or disappointment, lawful troubles, social disengagement, and physical sicknesses (counting hypochondriacal distraction), ordinarily are accounted for or seen in youngsters who endeavor suicide. These encouraging variables frequently are referred to by young people as purposes behind endeavoring suicide. Gay and indiscriminate teenagers have been accounted for to show high rates of despondency and have been recorded to have rates of Suicide bombing ideation and endeavors 3 times greater than other young people. Investigations of twins demonstrate that monozygotic twins indicate fundamentally higher concordance for suicide than dizygotic twins. Long haul significant amounts of group savagery may add to enthusiastic and lead issues and add to the danger of suicide for uncovered youth (Bergen, Hoffman & Tiedemann, 2011). Adolescent and parent polls that cover those risk variables recorded above might be valuable in the workplace setting to help with acquiring a total history. Suicide is an impressive general medical issue; more than 30 000 suicide killings in the United States and about 1 million suicide killings overall happen each year.

On a daily basis, our humanity is shoved into our faces by those who by the way they act and talk betray the whole essence of humanity. That aside, it is believed that the more we grow, the responsibility we accumulate, the more pressure we carry and the more the world leans on us, all these can be too much for a growing young man or woman. The pressure that they get are diverse, and they continue to expand and increase as these young men and women grow. The pressure may be from school, the need to excel in school. When a child is not doing

well enough in school, the pressure starts
coming from parents, teachers and sometimes
even friends, all these people wanting to
see the child perform better will
continually pile pressure on the kid. Those
around him, especially those older will
start talking about his / her other friends
that are doing well in school, comparing him
/ her to them. Sometimes, they never meet up,
and when they do not meet up, in spite of
the fact that they have tried, they start to
feel like a failure, like someone who can
never achieve any greatness in life. The
kids might start to feel like an outcast,
might start to find it difficult to blend in
among his/her pairs. At this point, the
child might start to get suicidal thoughts,
the might start to feel like it is totally
hopeless and futile to keep on living when
the handwriting of an imminent doom is
boldly on the wall, and sadly, some give in
to this thought.

Also, we have seen and we have extravagant
examples of kids that are doing well in
school, and still yet they commit suicide or
attempt to commit it. One would be forced to
seriously wonder what could be the reason
behind this. Research has shown that a lot

of teens contemplate suicide when they do not get enough support from the significant adults in their life, as such they feel isolated and therefore consider suicide as the only way out of their problems. And this seems to happen a lot, as a lot of times, the adults are also busy trying to keep their heads together, and trying to stay sane in a world that drives people crazy. A lot of adults unconsciously pay little attention to the little kids they have around, and this unbeknownst to them also, has a strong negative effect on the kids. Isolation and lack of attention is most felt by kids who most of the times keep to themselves, thereby having the adult as the only figure they may be close with. However, it doesn't affect only the recluse, it similarly affects kids who identify with others. The reason why normal kids commit suicide is not limited to isolation or lack of attention by the significant elders in their lives, worries and anxiety are factors of life that affects everyone regardless of age or success. That is why it can be seen that a successful businessman or an excellent kid in school commits suicide. The fear of the future and the pressure that comes with it is an important factor responsible for a lot of suicide attempts by kids and teenagers. A lot of times they feel worthless and therefore consider it unnecessary to continue to live.

Another reason why perfect kids who are high fliers in school, with great and affable personality get suicidal thoughts or even go all the way to commit suicide can be traced to family issues. Kids who come from troubled homes stand a greater risk of committing suicide than those who come from peaceful homes. Also, kids whose parents are either divorced or separated also stand a greater risk of committing suicide. Research by scholars has shown that when the family is together, members of the family are more relaxed and they stand a lower chance of committing suicide. Different scholars have explained that people who commit suicide do not usually get the idea just once, it is an ideation that keeps coming back to them. Sometimes, in fact, a lot of times they try to push it away. At this point, if the individual gets help, they can survive and live through that face. However, if they do not get help, the thought will eventually overwhelm them until it is too loud to ignore. The reason why people from loving and peaceful families stand a higher chance of not committing suicide is because, at the point where the individual is struggling with a lot of personal issues, there is a higher chance that it will be noticed by someone in the family. People who commit suicide often show signs of that characterize the troubling phase they are going through, and they often engage in activities such as; alcohol, drugs, withdrawal, signs of depression, etc. When this happens, individuals who share deep family bonds are more likely to get out of it as their struggles will be easily noticed by other members of their family. However, divorce doesn't only have effects on the parents, it most of the times also has a telling effect on the children, as they are cut off from one of their parents. This physical distance joined with other psychological issues make the children also stand the risk of suicide in a divorce situation. As stated above, children from separated homes have been said to have more cases of attempted and successful suicide than those who live with both of their parents.

People who have just lost a loved one or who have just gotten out of a relationship also show more signs of suicidal actions. A recent study carried out by the National Institute for Healthcare in Rockville, MD indicates that divorced people are three times as likely to commit suicide as people who are married. The institute says that divorce now ranks as the number one factor linked with suicide rates in major US cities, ranking above all other physical, financial and psychological factors (divorceinfo.com). Also a research conducted by the regional European office of the World Health Organization across 13 countries found that divorce was the only factor that was present in suicide cases in all the countries, that is, divorce was the only factor linked with suicide in all the 13 countries. Separation from relationships is also as bad as divorce, as partners also share a bond similar to that of married people. Many studies have revealed that women who just got divorced are more likely to attempt suicide than men, but statistically, men are more likely to succeed. This is so as a result of the fact that a lot of men get hit by the fact that they are no longer the head of the house, therefore they feel less needed. Women however feel more needed after divorce because of the fact that they had children to care for, so the most times try to transfer their attention to their children.

The pressure that affects adults quite varies and it is often widespread. A lot of conditions come together to form the pressure that an adult feel. The first being the pressure to succeed. Immediately an individual crosses the big teenage line, and he/she finishes college, the pressure to succeed becomes a pressing aspect of their psychological factor which they have to battle with. Every child grows up with high hopes and aspiration. Some were merely lofty ambitions; others were realistic dreams which the dreamer works actively towards. With age and growth, it becomes increasingly essential for them to live out this dream, however, most often than none, they get frustrated by the economic and political system. It becomes more excruciating when they start to see their friends or pears who have made it within a short period of time. At this point, it starts to dawn on people that they are far behind their mates and this can arouse a suicidal thought. The fact that their mates, who they used to be the

same with or those they had grown up are
with are no doing so well, while they are
still struggling is also very important.
This makes the individual feel like a
failure and thus a prime candidate for
suicide.

Closely related to this is the expectation
that is placed on young men and women.
Youths, especially those around the age
grade of 25-40 have a lot of expectation
placed on their shoulder by the society,
their family and by friends and family. The
inability of an individual to meet this
expectation may result to the person
counting him/herself a loser and a failure.
A lot of times, the society dictates our
movement across life, sometimes we have a
different route to journey through, but life
takes us through another route and also
places expectation on us. The immediate
family of people is also an important reason
for this. They pile pressure upon pressure
on the individual, unbeknownst to them, this
pressure rarely does anything in become
successful or achieve that which they want
to achieve, it instead, it makes them
consider their lives a waste and therefore

think of suicide as the only solution to such problem.

Another form of pressure which is often felt by adults is the pressure that comes from having a family, and having to fend for that family. Either of men and women or even both can feel the pressure that comes from family. Sometimes it can be the pressure to keep the family together, some other times it might be the pressure from the other spouse, a lot of times all these accumulate and result in suicidal thoughts.

Stress is another factor which is closely related to pressure. The accumulation of stress from work place from home and other places is considered to be a huge factor responsible for quite a number of suicides. This factor is also believed to be job related to a very large extent. It is believed that those in the medical profession stand a higher chance to commit suicide due to stress. Among those in the medical line, dentists are believed to be at a higher risk to die from suicide. This believe is largely speculative, however, some scholars have ventured to carry out a research on this factor and have come to varying conclusions. One of such scholars is Roger E. Alexander, who in a paper he published, was able to state the result of a result he carried out among dental practitioners. He was able to gather that more dentists do not really commit suicide more than people from other fields, he however, was able to gather that there seems to be a higher percentage of female dentists committing suicide than in any other field. He however believes that the available data were insufficient to guarantee an exclusive research.

Scholars have also identified workplace as an increasing factor for attempted suicides and successful suicides. There is a higher risk of individuals who are employed in a workplace that is not very active to commit suicide than those that work in busy environment. Redundancy has been identified as a reason why a lot of people commit suicide. People tend to be more engaged in an active work environment and when they are engaged, the possible of suicide has been reduced. Also, people have previously been injured in a workplace have been discovered to be victims of workplace suicide more than those who have experienced no previous workplace injury. Workplace bully has also been identified as a major reason why a lot of people commit suicide. Just like normal teenage bully, workplace bully is a very bad and dangerous act that can lead to such bitter ends like suicide.

Factors like legal troubles and physical sickness are also believed to be important factors that lead to suicide. People who have legal cases are also believed to get suicidal ideations more than those who have no legal trouble. This happens especially in the case of people who have serious cases, but have had no prior criminal records. Also people who are believed to be noble men or held high in the society are also believed to result to suicide in other to safe themselves from the looming embarrassment. A lot of those who have previously been held has holy or pious men who get charged often commit suicide even after they have been released, as they can barely stand the scorn that they will be subjected too by people. Similarly, people who have been wrongly arrested and convicted of a crime they never committed have also been said to result to suicide in other to avoid the looming punishment for a crime they did not commit.

While all these reasons are legal and lawful factors responsible for suicide, a lot of people commit suicide for legal reasons that are not as complex or tough as the above listed. Similarly, people who have been diagnosed with terminal diseases have also been identified as being more likely to commit suicide than individuals who are in perfect health. This as a result of a lot of them giving up already. A lot of them knowing that death is imminent already prefer to die immediately and not subject themselves to the torture that sometimes accompanies such death. People with one physical sickness have also been identified to be prone to committing suicide. Same with those who have had a part of their body as a result of accident or those who have completely lost the use some parts of their body.

One very important factor that leads young men and women to suicide is the societal perception of who they are, and how the society sees and accepts them. This is a very important factor that often gets overlooked. A lot of people battle with coming to terms with who they are and how the society accepts them for it. A lot of people get taunted and bullied for who they are and how they look. One of the major cause of suicide among teen ladies is the size of their body and how they look. Teenagers while just coming to terms with who they are and how they look become very sensitive to how people around them think they look. A lot of times teenagers want validation from people that they are beautiful and that they look good. When those from whom they seek validation think they do not look good enough, it often demoralizes them and often leads to series of unpalatable reactions such as depression and withdrawal. These incidents when not properly managed quickly lead suicidal thoughts and attempts.

Similarly, physical structures such as fatness often get gibed by people. Often times the society has a stereotyped way of viewing events, that when things do not go that way, or when anyone does not conform to their standard, they consider the person a misfit and subject such a person to unimaginable ridicule. A lot of times this often degenerate into unwanted situations for the individuals involved. A lot of times, the teenagers that fall into this prey are

people just looking to be accepted for who
they are. The differences which these
individuals portray maybe something small
and inconsequential as the way they dress,
the way they walk, the way they talk, and
other such seemingly trivial and unimportant
details. With this factor leading to lot of
teenage deaths, consciousness has been
raised towards it, ferocious campaign
launched against it, but it has shown no
sign of pausing or slowing down at the
moment. With this, a lot of teenagers
continue to fall prey of the situation,
oblivious of it. Teenagers who often fall
into this situation are fat girls, and they
get gibed for how fat they are and how their
body looks. A lot of oversize teenagers
often find it difficult to fit in or to
blend like the rest of the pears, as they
often get gibed for everything and whatever
they do or wear. Research has shown that
oversized ladies, especially teenagers, are
more likely to commit suicide than ladies
who are considered to be the normal without
any physical impediment. This is an
unbelievable factor that is responsible for
the rise in the number of teenage death.
Though ladies are most affected by this, it
is not limited to ladies alone, as everyone

struggles with different societal issues. Ladies are not the only ones who are over-size, a lot of men experience such gibes.

## Cyber Space Inspiring Suicide Bombers

The part that the Internet, especially online networking, may have in suicide-related conduct is a point of developing interest and debate. The current increment in profoundly plugged instances of suicide that include web-based social networking has attracted national consideration regarding this theme Researchers are additionally inspired by whether the Internet all-in-all principally aides or thwarts suicide anticipation. Endeavors to evaluate the degree of the Internet's impact on suicide conduct are difficult in view of the roundabout and complex relationship between Internets utilize and suicide (Kroenig & Pavel, 2012).

## Suicide Bomber Based on Long Term Effects from Savagery of War

Fighting forever and survival, attempting to achieve a goal, is one of the essential qualities of human instinct. People frequently utilize brutality to achieve their objectives. Savagery can be systematized or not, sorted out or not, and it is one of the attributes which makes human violence not quite the same as the brutality found in nature; it is the longing of society to legitimize these demonstrations. The most noteworthy and most complex type of human intercommunity brutality is called war. There are chosen groups of individuals who dedicate their lives to war and violence as a component of their day to day life (Bergen, Hoffman & Tiedemann, 2011).

Ultimately, it could be said that finding an individual at their low moment in life and recruiting them to conduct a suicide bombing would not be very challenging.

# REFERENCES

Alvanou, M. (2008). Palestinian women suicide bombers: The interplaying effects of Islam, nationalism and honor culture. Homeland Security Rev., 2, 1.

Antonius, D. (2013). The political psychology of terrorism fears. Oxford University Press.

Asad, T. (2007). On suicide bombing. Columbia University Press.

Asensio, J. A., & Trunkey, D. D. (2008). Current therapy of trauma and surgical critical care. Elsevier Health Sciences.

Atran, S. (2003). Genesis of suicide terrorism. Science, 299(5612), 1534-1539.

Benmelech, E., & Berrebi, C. (2007). Human capital and the productivity of suicide bombers. The Journal of Economic Perspectives, 21(3), 223-238.

Bergen, P., Hoffman, B., & Tiedemann, K. (2011). Assessing the Jihadist terrorist threat to America and American interests. Studies in Conflict & Terrorism, 34(2), 65-101.

Bergholz, M. (2016). Rory Yeomans, The Utopia of terror: life and death in wartime Croatia.

Bukay, D. (2017). The Religious Foundations of Suicide Bombings. Middle East Forum. Retrieved 21 January 2017, from http://www.meforum.org/1003/the-religious- foundations of-suicide-bombings

Clapper, J. C. (2013). Worldwide threat assessment of the US intelligence community. OFFICE OF THE DIRECTOR OF NATIONAL INTELLIGENCE WASHINGTON DC.

Coady, C. A. (2004). Terrorism, morality, and supreme emergency. Ethics, 114(4), 772-789.

Connors, T. P., & Pellegrini, G. (2005). Hard lessons won: Policing terrorism in the United States. Safe Cities Project, the Manhattan Institute, 5.

Cordesman, A. H. (1997). US forces in the Middle East: resources and capabilities. Westview Pr.

Cordesman, A. H., & Hashim, A. (1997). Iran: dilemmas of dual containment. Westview Pr.

Crain, N. V., & Crain, W. M. (2006). Terrorized economies. Public Choice, 128(1), 317-349.

Dahl, E. J. (2011). The plots that failed: Intelligence lessons learned from unsuccessful terrorist attacks against the United States. Studies in Conflict & Terrorism, 34(8), 621-648.

Discover Policing. (n.d.). Retrieved from http://discoverpolicing.org/whats_like/?fa=types_jobs

Drinkwine, B. M., & Army War College (U.S.). (2008).The serpent in our garden: Al-Qa'ida and the long war. Carlisle Barracks, Pa: U.S. Army War College.

Egner, M. (2009). Social-Science Foundations for Strategic Communications in the Global War on Terrorism. Social Science for Counterterrorism, 74(06-C), 323.

Espejo, R. (2009). What motivates suicide bombers? Detroit, MI: Greenhaven Press.

FBI Academy, Quantico & Virginia. (2002). Countering Terrorism: Integration of Practice and Theory. University of Pennsylvania

Forest, J. J. F. (2007). Countering terrorism and insurgency in the 21st century: International perspectives. Westport, Conn. [u.a.:Praeger Security International.

Heaton, R. (2000). The prospects for intelligence- led policing: Some historical and quantitative considerations. Policing and Society: An International Journal, 9(4), 337-355.

Hoffman, B. (2003). The Logic of Suicide Terrorism. The Atlantic, June 2003 issue

Innes, M. (2004). Reinventing tradition? Reassurance, neighborhood security and policing. Criminal Justice, 4(2), 151-171.

Kelling, G., & Bratton, W. (2006). Policing terrorism, civic bulletin 43. New York: Manhattan Institute for Policy Research.

Khatib, L., Matar, D., & Alshaer, A. (2014). The Hizbullah phenomenon: Politics and communication.

Khosrokhavar, F. (2005). Suicide bombers: Allah's new martyrs. Pluto Press (UK).

Kimhi, S., & Even, S. (2004). Who are the Palestinian suicide bombers? Terrorism and Political Violence, 16(4), 815-840.

Kroenig, M., & Pavel, B. (2012). How to deter terrorism. The Washington Quarterly, 35(2), 21-36.

Kulick, A. (2009). Israel's confrontation with suicide terrorism. In O. Falk and H. Morgenstern (Eds.). Suicide terror: Understanding and confronting the threat (pp. 73-157). Hoboken, N.J.:Wiley & Sons, Inc.

Lambertus, S., & Yakimchuk, R. (2007). Future of Policing in Alberta: International Trends and Case Studies.

Lankford, A. (2013). A comparative analysis of suicide terrorists and rampage, workplace, and school shooters in the United States from 1990 to 2010. Homicide Studies, 17(3), 255-274.

Lennquist, S. (Ed.). (2012). Medical response to major incidents and disasters: a practical guide for all medical staff. Springer Science & Business Media.

Lester, D., Yang, B., & Lindsay, M. (2004). Suicide bombers: Are psychological profiles possible? Studies in Conflict & Terrorism, 27(4), 283-295.

Malik, J. M. (2002). Dragon on terrorism: assessing China's tactical gains and strategic losses after 11 September. Contemporary Southeast Asia, 252-293.

Merari, A., & Friedland, N. (1985). Social psychological aspects of political terrorism. Applied social psychology annual, 6, 185-205.

Metzger, J. (2006). Preventing terrorist bombings on United States subway systems (Doctoral dissertation, Monterey, California. Naval Postgraduate School).

Morgenstern, H. (2009). The global jihad. In O. Falk and H. Morgenstern (Eds.). Suicide terror: Understanding and confronting the threat (pp. 31-68). Hoboken, N.J.: Wiley & Sons, Inc.

Morgenstern, H., & Falk, O. (2009). Suicide terror: Understanding and confronting the threat. Hoboken, N.J: Wiley.

National Commission on Terrorist Attacks Upon the United States, (2004). The 9/11 Commission Report: Final Report of the National Commission on Terrorist Attacks Upon the United States. Available at: www.9-11commission.gov/report/911Report_Exec.htm

NATO Advanced Training Course on Future Trends and New Approaches in Defeating the Terrorism Threat, In Gürbüz, U., & IOS Press. (2013). Future trends and new approaches in defeating the terrorism threat.

O 'Rourke, L.A. (2009). What's special about female suicide terrorism? Security Studies, 18, 681-   718.doi:10.1080/09636410903369084

Olson, D. T. (2012). Tactical counterterrorism: The law enforcement manual of terrorism prevention. Springfield, Ill: Charles C. Thomas.

Pape, R. (2005). Dying to win: The strategic logic of suicide terrorism. Melbourne: Scribe.

Pedahzur, A. (2005). Suicide terrorism. Polity.

Pellegrini, G. & Connors, T., (2005). Hard Won Lessons: Policing Terrorism In The United States. Safe Cities Project Manhattan Institute For Policy Research 52 Vanderbilt Avenue • New York, NY

Pham, J. P. (2012). Boko Haram's evolving threat. Africa security briefs, (20), 1.

Pierre, J. (2017). Culturally sanctioned suicide: Euthanasia, seppuku, and terrorist martyrdom. PubMed Central (PMC). Retrieved 21 January 2017, from https://www.ncbi.nlm.nih.gov/pmc/articles/PMC4369548/

Rakhra, K. (2008). Suicide terrorism (Jul-Dec 2007). Institute for Peace and Conflict Studies Special Report, 55.

Religion. (2011) In Merriam-Webster Online Dictionary. Retrieved from http//:www.merriam/webster.com/dictionary/religion

Reuter, C. (2004). My life is a weapon: A modern history of suicide bombing. Princeton: Princeton Univ. Press.

Richman, A., Shapira, S. C., & Sharan, Y. (2010). Medical response to terror threats. Amsterdam: IOS Prss.

Richman, A., & Sharan, Y. (Eds.). (2015). Lone Actors–An Emerging Security Threat (Vol. 123). IOS Press.

Sage, A. L. (2011, July). The evolving threat of Al Qaeda in the Islamic Maghreb. In Strategic Forum (No. 268, p. 1). National Defense University.

Shahar, Y. (2002). The al-Aqsa Martyrs Brigades - A political tool with an edge. International Institute for Counter-Terrorism. Retrieved from http://www.ict.org.il/Articles/tabid/66/Articlsid/78/currentpage/18/Default.aspx

Skaine, R. (2013). Suicide warfare: Culture, the military, and the individual as a weapon. Santa Barbara, Calif: Praeger

Stork, J. (2002). Erased in a moment: Suicide bombing attacks against Israeli civilians: [Israel, occupied West Bank and Gaza Strip, Palestinian Authority Territories]. New York [u.a.: Human Rights Watch.

Studios, A. C. H., & by Cricketdiane, G. N. M. G. Daily Archives: September 19, 2009.

Timothy p. Connors. (2005). Hard won lessons: policing terrorism in the United States. Georgia Pellegrini

Weinberg, L., Pedahzur, A., & Canetti-Nisim, D. (2003). The social and religious characteristics of suicide bombers and their victims. Terrorism and Political Violence, 15(3), 139-153.

Wicker, B. (2006). Witnesses to faith? The concept of martyrdom in Christianity and Islam. Aldershot [u.a.: Ashgate

Vaknin, S. (2004). Terrorists and Freedom Fighters. Narcissus Publications.

Victoroff, J. (2005). The mind of the terrorist: A review and critique of psychological approaches. Journal of Conflict resolution, 49(1), 3-42.

## Image credit:

News Direct, (Sept 23, 2014). Iraq violence: Suicide bomber detonates explosive vest inside Shi'ite bomb, kills 15. https://www.youtube.com/watch?v=w_Q5B8AJvsI

News Direct, (May 29, 2014). Scores of early voters killed by Iraqi suicide bombers. https://www.youtube.com/watch?v=qWD68nDiv8A

Patrick T. Fallon, (June 16, 2013). Los Angeles, CA-IN PHOTOS: LAPD Holds Downtown Counterterrorism Drill. REUTERS. http://www.vosizneias.com/132695/2013/06/07/los-angeles-ca-in-photos-lapd-holds-downtown-counterterrorism-drill/

Wally Z., How to Make Arduino Police Lights. http://www.instructables.com/id/How-to-make-Arduino-Police-Lights/

Made in the USA
Middletown, DE
31 December 2020